Splendorous Light Within

SPLENDOROUS
Light Within

By

Lachlen Paul French

Event Horizon Publishing ltd

With the exception of small passages quoted for review purposes, this edition may not be reproduced, translated, adapted, copied, stored in a retrieval system or transmitted in any form or through any means including mechanical, electronic, photocopying or otherwise without the permission of the publisher here and the author Lachlen Paul French.

2011 ® Registered Writer's Guild West
© Lachlen French 2011

United States Copyright Office
1-639784961

ISBN-13: 978-0615538693
(Event Horizon Publishing ldt)

ISBN-10: 061553869X

Go to:
http://www.booksinthelight.com

for Glenda…

for the Deepest Love

In this "elevated depth" within .. a Vibrational Permeation deeply penetrates us ... and purifies our old self images of their coherence ... their cohesion.

Sublime Oneness

There is a vast unplumbed inner world .. that we may find,
that we may reach ... haply, haltingly, yet gracefully ...
that when visited, exults our being .. in shared Auras;
Yet our sensibilities are Dismayed as well.

In this "elevated depth" within .. a Vibrational Permeation
deeply penetrates us .. and purifies our old self images
of their coherence .. their cohesion. And our Identity herein,
becomes Pure Unfettered Simplicity – of being.

This vast Inner experience restores to us 'Knowing our Heritage'
   (as in a dream .. faintly remembered).
It energizes a Deep Awarenesses in us .. of our Eternity,
and grants us Feelings ... that ne'er were touched.
The amplification In and Of our Being ...
in this rarefied Knowing,
lights ancient memories of our Original SELF
(as an identity from above) .. somewhere .. somehow.

Yet .. finally, we are Hollowed out .. we are Emptied;
but we are filled with a glory of some Heavenly Sun,
.. barely seen later, in the "afterglows remembered."
But we DO Remember feeling absolute Surrender in the face of
an All Consuming Love; And we feel an unyielding deferential Awe
in wordless jubilation .. that we've even FELT such Tenderness.

Forever After we are changed.
We are always looking for its surprises around endless corners,
over hills .. in other fields and byways.
We Often feel its marbled essence and apparitions,
maybe Here, maybe There, and Yonder... and often at night.
YES feeling it, sensing it, it is like a fond invisible touch on our skin
or a lovely Aromatic Essence – a sort of ever-present FRAGRANCE
Of Grace .. blessing our Awareness .. Promising its next visitation.

It's felt especially in our deeply conscious breath and breathing,
for OUR breath, is ITS etheric Essence -- Invisible, Powerful.

Yes, it actually Permeates our being .. AS Our Being;
   (being only .. a Consciousness of Loving Life).
So finally .. never releasing its Love .. we also become,
its Compassioned and Passionate Ambassador.

Foreword

Splendorous Light Within is truly a vibrant comprehensive presentation covering vast spiritual territory. Its breadth and depth are remarkable. Some of this terrain may be new for readers, but some is not, as Lachlen Paul French covers spiritual technologies and ancient unknown mystical truths that parlay now, into modern day sensibilities and practice. Translating ancient principles into a current frame of reference, for our modern minds, helps greatly.

His viewpoint comes from years of spiritual study, exploration and experiential work. He's a scout – an explorer who ventured forth into unmapped territory and sends 'back to our civilization his maps, rough sketches and insights.' The poem on page 7 reveals such a promise for us. Joined with our personal experiences, *our* faith and our willingness to also venture forward, we find our own glorious knowing and freedom, reading this book.

I enjoy how he so plainly shares quantum physics as a basis of God's energetic universe, and relates it to the mysteries of Light and Sound. It finally makes sense. By comprehending such a fascinating interior world, in easy sharing, he unveils the meaning of scientific ideas that are unknown to many. Then with this insight he irrefutably dislodges old-fashioned theories on *haphazard accidental* evolution, along with other generally accepted nonsense, which in truth have never even been tested. In presenting quantum physic's elegant beauty as a foundation in all the universe, he shows how Darwin's 'random haphazardness' could never fit into the prime moving science and ever-present mathematic formulae that are everywhere within the cosmos, even in its structure. The universe is so miraculously mathematic, down to the ratio of force inside of all atoms, quadrillions of dumb luck *accidents* could never be our beginning. He gives a more updated discourse that merges spirituality and science naturally. This unification is all important.

It is now intellectually satisfying to finally learn about the Essene teachings whose Jewish spiritual sect Christ was raised within, as seen in their scrolls; and to also learn about the Gnostics, as well as the *biblical code-language* which most have never heard of, and to read a translation of the *Gospel of Thomas* – that gospel found in desert sand in 1945 after being lost for two millennia. It's like listening to Christ speak directly to us. Knowing Christ's sect was the third primary Path of his day, finally makes sense.

I draw more inspiration from the words here that *attention equals faith*. It reveals how we may apply our daily energy to matters of conscious or transformational growth. I feel gratitude and awe as God's nature is illuminated *within* our own nature, and it is shared here, how in the intimacy of our oneness with God, we co-create a life worth living — *in* the awareness of the Divine presence within *our* being.

The author's explanation of how the word *Breath* has been inaccurately translated into the Latin word *'Spirit'* in the Old and New Testaments is also an amazing revelation, *unknown* by almost everyone anywhere. This one fact when known, changes almost everything we may believe we understand about the ancient spiritual truths. The spirit-Breath is *God-breathed light-energy within us* – our divine ability – and it is what was given to the new believers as mentioned in the book of Acts. For me this really is *God-breathed divine ability* belonging to each of us. I can share now that *Splendorous Light Within* covers a wealth of territory in such an engaging fashion, it's truly a classroom in and of itself. This book here so aptly follows his previous book, *Breath of Light*.

I'm a fan of the quote: "*All Instruction is but a Finger-Pointing to the Moon. Those whose gaze is fixed upon the Pointer, will never see beyond it. Let him catch even a sight of the moon, and still he cannot see its beauty*".

In truth, it has to be our own *awareness* and *practice* of spiritual principles that bring about personal revelation – laying the foundation for our own full life. Coming to know our oneness with the Divine, our co-creative ability is the path of Light that Lachlen Paul French shares with us here.

I think of Lachlen as someone who's actually 'been to the moon and back' having been infused by that light; the ever-present light in each of us. It's our **Splendorous Light Within.** Let him share all of it with you... right here and right now.

Forward by Barbara Patton Unger, author of...**Salvation Rocks**: *Rescued, Rooted and Co-Creating Your Wonderful Life..* and, **Taste the Grace**: *How God's Love Empowers Us to Feel Good, Do Good and Make Good.*

- INTRODUCTION -

Recently tremendous new scientific and historic facts have arisen regarding humanity's story, which most people have frankly never heard before. It's now so exciting, many feel we are in a new golden age. Information has risen exponentially in recent years, so *new views* abound essentially in every discipline and science. We can actually say that what we believed decades ago, has not only become undeveloped old information, but now is turned-over, transformed, or may be fully contradicted.

Metaphysical-spiritual awareness is also enhanced, amplified and altered by the newest advanced findings. Archeological, historic, linguistic, and scientific data, with brand new discoveries on the ancient times and people (far preceding standard views that Sumeria began human civilization 4000 BC) has truly transformed our understanding of what preceded our civilization. Formerly, we were supposed to believe that only stone-age cavemen preceded Sumeria. Yet the new researchers (*knowing the new facts*) along with those who employ them, as well as a special few with whom they share — are the only ones *aware* of the new transformations regarding former historical beliefs. If you are not seeking out this new data in perhaps arcane periodicals, or searching the book shelves for the most recent advanced research you will not have learned about any of these matters, or their implications for understanding history, or where we came from. Because academia, which loves Darwin, is controlled by a *jealous few* and because they have a value-system of keeping well-worn time-bound views deeply in place, it allows them a luxury of remaining as upper level authorities on what is true, for Truth. They essentially keep the newest facts *challenging* old views out of awareness, out of print, or both. Only when something is truly *shocking* may it escape the confines of this jealous world getting out to the media (which has its own agenda) to make a wider audience *excited* that something new has been discovered.

We now know *scientifically* that our human DNA as 'Homo Sapien' is from 200,000 years ago. It did not exist here prior. This human *chapter* has now developed into a modern form, but it has had several chapters before our time often referred to as ancient civilizations (*which we're not supposed to know about*). Amazingly, their **ancient sciences** are now often seen to be advanced over our sciences today (i.e. *building the pyramids).* For example the ancient city-civilization under the Indian Ocean, just off

India's southern beaches, reveals an amazing advanced kingdom *predating* Sumeria – by 12-15,000 years – which looks to have been destroyed by advanced fire-weapons from above. Also, the Sphinx in Egypt is now known to have water-erosion in *wearing-down* its stone in Vertical patterns. Those cracks and creases reveal that water, not wind or sand truly eroded, or aged the Sphinx. The last time water rained down on the Sahara area was 50,000 years ago. To wear it down that way, the Sphinx must have been rained on for thousands of years. The Sphinx and Pyramids are far older than a few thousand years, as has been told us.

Spirituality on Earth from the first (*taught by Christ in his Essene mission*) gave this pure ancient knowledge to our cultures (coming from long *before* Abraham, who was one of the *'water-bearers'* of that original Light). The poly-theistic chapters or cultures of human religion (with Gods of war, fire, fertility, crops and the sea) and the demi-gods of Greek, Egyptian, Dogon, South Pacific, Maya, Hopi or Chinese mythologies, as well as the scattered European people – were actually a lower version of a once higher purer awareness. Gods of wood, stone, gold or onyx were where humanity went to when we fell into a sort of unconsciousness. In this book we refer to The Divine in purest terms; and in both male and female terms, because the Divine is *both* energies. Terms like *'He Who Is'* is here from the Hebrew YHVH, *God* is too and *Father Within,* from Christ. *Divine Being* and *Divine One, Infinite Invisible, The One, Her* and *His* are seen; *He and She* are used and *Father or Mother* are too. The one that you prefer is used generously herein. So, it seems humanity starts out with pure knowledge, and then we forget, get lost, or completely lose our connection with a more excellent *past* awareness, that we once enjoyed. We now know from studying the records of these past civilizations, they *All write* that they were lifted up and educated by Beings from the Sky or the Water, who had a benevolent educational attitude toward all of us.

Earth is our present home, school-ground and recreation area. We are not *Who* or *What* we may believe we are. Pseudo science like *Darwin's* is proven fully wrong now, right here in this book. The excitement is now in your hands. If you wanted release from unease, fear or gnawing ego-identifications (as well as its ignorance) **Splendorous Light Within** is here for You and yours. Read blissfully to lift up your mind and heart.

LIFE - LIVING - CONSCIOUSNESS

"THE DAYS OF OUR YEARS HERE, ARE "THREE-SCORE YEARS AND TEN" AND IF BY REASON OF OUR STRENGTH, THEY BECOME 'FOUR SCORE YEARS' STILL THERE IS ALWAYS STRENGTH, LABOR AND SORROW THEN IT IS SOON CUT OFF

AND THEN .. WE FLY AWAY..."   PSALM 90:10

"FOR WHEN WE SHALL RISE FROM DEATH, WE NEITHER MARRY, NOR ARE GIVEN IN MARRIAGE...AND ALSO AS CONCERNING THE DEAD, THAT THEY RISE UP, HAVE YOU NOT READ IN MOSES' BOOK, HOW IN THE BUSH, GOD SPOKE TO HIM SAYING:

"I AM THE GOD OF ABRAHAM, THE GOD OF ISAAC, THE GOD OF JACOB". HE IS NOT THE GOD OF THE DEAD, BUT THE GOD OF THE LIVING.

YOU THEREFORE DO GREATLY ERR.   MARK 12:25-27

"YOU CAME INTO THE WORLD UNFETTERED..
AND YOU SHALL LEAVE THE WORLD UNFETTERED."

THOMAS' GOSPEL VS. 28

~ *The Ancient* "Emerald Tablet" ~
(In the Beginning
...and even Now)

What is Below (the human expression)
is like that Above (the Divine Source).
What is Above (the Heavenly Creative Consciousness),
is Similar, to That below (the subservient Earthly Manifestation)
…to accomplish the wonders of The One.
As all things were produced by
the mediation of The One Being,
So all things were produced from The One…
in continuing adaptation.
It is the cause of all Perfection throughout…
Separate the Earth (the bodily identification)
from the Fire (the elevating Breath)
And segregate the Subtle (the Soul's Vision)
from the Gross, (from the ego-persona)
and act Prudently (holding serenely In Consciousness, Your Truth).
Then, with Discernment, Ascend with the greatest Sagacity,
From the Earth (from your lower earthly perspective)
Up to Heaven (up to your Creative, Heavenly Consciousness)
And then… with Resolution… descend again to Earth.

UNITE together the power of things inferior, with SUPERIOR…
Thus… you will possess the Light of the whole world…
And all Obscurity will fly away from you.
(*All Untoward Conditions and Confusion will Melt Away from your life*).
This Knowledge has more Fortitude than fortitude itself,
because it will overcome every subtle thing (every causal force)…
and it will Penetrate… every solid thing
(all material manifestations).
By This path, the world was formed."

Adapted from — The Emerald Tablet of '*Hermes Trismagistus*' – aka: Enoch
(parentheses are mine, bold is the original)

SPLENDOROUS Light Within
(KABALA ZOHAR YOGA)

TABLE OF CONTENTS
PAGE

SUBLIME ONENESS 7

FOREWORD. 8

INTRODUCTION. 10

THE EMERALD TABLET – IN THE
BEGINNING & EVEN NOW. 13

I. KABALA ZOHAR YOGA 17
    In the Beginning, Spirituality Was Before Religion 23

II. PRESENT KNOWLEDGE 31
    Becoming Divinely Human. 33
    Divine Mind Shines in 'Everything'. 35
    From Bliss...Into the Earth. 37

III. THE PAIN OF 'ME' LEADS US TO
OUR DIVINE PARTNERSHIP 41

IV. THE DIMENSION OF INFINITE
MIND BINDS EVERYTHING 45

    If We Do Not See Divine Brilliance
        Everywhere, We Do Not Really See 54
    Living With What Is, And Improving It 59
    The Total Reality Within Consciousness 61

V. A PATH UPWARD 69

    That Which is Called Prayer 70
    When Praying 71
    Our Divine BREATH – One-With *The One* 73
    The Uniqueness of Jesus' Teaching 78
    Creating the New Human Being. 81
    The Promise of 'The Dominion of Heaven' in Your Life 87
    Jesus' Quotation – from – *The Secret Book of John* 90
    Essene Worship Poetry 92

The Gospel According to Thomas

Amplified and Interpreted for Today

Table of Contents

Chapter Title	Page
1. The Decision: to Journey Back to the Light	99
2. Leaving the World Behind	115
3. The Growth of the Inner Child	123
4. The Path of Grace: Friendship with the Divine	129
5. The Path of Ascension: *Uniting Spirituality with the Outer Life*	135
6. Living Amid the Challenges and Tests	145
7. Reunification: Your Discipline and Destination	151
8. The Kingdom of Heaven: *Our Ever-Expanding Expansive Awareness*	159
9. Living Daily the Life of Transformation	169
10. The Temptation: Whose Temple is It?	179
11. The Solitary One: *In the Light*	187
Page /Verse Locator	194-195
Quotations in "Thomas"	194-195
Sacred Power For Purification and Elevation	197

The One pondered beyond the Void and the
Emptiness; beyond the darkness;
beyond the stillness, for the purpose
of making a Divine Family...

I. Kabala Zohar Yoga

"Receiving Splendorous-Union"
Spiritual Science
Love Shared
I AM
I

Before the beginning of universal Spiritual-Energy and Matter,
Creative Divine Meditation .. transpired.
Stillness and darkness permeated this meditation,
so *The One* could ponder all things in pure clarity.
All things were pondered by *The One* .. in an emptiness;
in a void of any Thing. The void was all.
The clarity was perfect. It was unmoving infinite solitude.

The One was and still *is* Alone in this state of infinite clarified
potentiality, and will always Know this place. But it is alloyed
in pure Consciousness, Being Itself the All, the Blackness, the Light,
and the No Thing, extended Out to the ancillary fields of Infinity
— where no border, boundary or 'edge' have existence.
The One is the *Designer* and *Emanator* of all dimensions, all vibrations,
all frequencies, all energy and all matter.
Splendorous Light was conceived in a Void [*of darkness, light and color*].

But *The One* pondered beyond the Void and the Emptiness;
beyond the darkness; beyond the stillness, for the purpose
of making a Divine Family – making an infinite Multitude
out of its own, infinite Conscious Essence.
Now Its own Divine essence – Its Creative Consciousness –
was all The One needed to create and manifest Its infinite Ideas.
Consider: how can we conceive of Music being imagined from silence?
God imagined 'Sound' in absolute Silent stillness ?? Yes.
How could that BE? When pondered, it's just unimaginable.
This is a Miracle of incomprehensible incredible Consciousness.
And how God invented Humor in infinite quiet, I just don't know.

Also movement was conceived in the presence of infinite Stillness.
This .. was also a miracle. The One imagined "throughness."
It went beyond *Hereness* in its Oneness, to the idea of over "There."
This too was Inexplicable.
The first Sound imagined — *a living Breath* — also initiated
an infinite yet minute cosmic *Pulse* (heartbeat and stillness) in this
infinite Infinitude. These also were Miracles in Imagination…
within formless, empty, pure Infinite Light-Consciousness.

The conception of a Partner — The Other — was also miraculous.
The Other, was .. *IS the Receiving half of The One*, 'receiving' the
Creative Ideas of The original One; to become the Giver of another
— the Progenitor of the Many.   The One Imagined with substantial
Consciousnes, Self as Many for The Mother, to birth local awareness.
Thus was family conceived. Perhaps the greatest benevolent miracle of
all .. was Apportioning Consciousness in Units — in you, me, all of us.
Individualized Consciousness in Portions arose.
Out of clarified aloneness came a Yearning from Solitude.
Out of yearning came partnership — Companionship.
Out of companionship and imagining came Family.
The One 'became' The Many through The Other.
Out of darkness and silence came the musical joy of Togetherness
the familial 'Light of Splendor.'
'Kabala-Zohar' IS "*Receiving the Splendorous Light Within*".

And when married to the power of Sound we have a universe
of Time and Space in Harmony – Miraculous Existence with
Sound and Light .. born out of Mind .. in incredible Ideation.
Out of Invisibility came Visibility.
In imagining infinitely small particles of Light, in a void
[*in Consciousness*] Essence became possible.
The particles were put together for a bonding and building use.
Out of emptiness came a fullness of Resplendent Consciousness…
…manifesting as glowing Light Substance (an Essence of bonding).
Out of stillness came the Breath - Sound.
Out of the breath-sound came Light 'Activity'.
Out of activity comes Movement. From movement came Rest.

I. Kabala Zohar Yoga

Out of rest comes Creativity.
Out of creativity comes Manifestation ...
(as Vibration and Rhythm) Time, Frequency, Music and Speech.
From manifestation comes the All.
From the All come Universal-Dimensions
Out of Universal Dimensions come Light and Darkness together —
side-by-side — as opposites, in a negative space and a positive space,
balancing each other.

Without Darkness as a background how can Light be appreciated?
Without Silence as background how can Sound be appreciated?
Without Motionlessness as background .. can we know Movement?
The Divine One is *I*nfinite motionless, silent creative Consciousness
Infinite *Above, Below,* infinite *East-West* across, and on infinite *angles.*
But Divine Being knew Motion needed To BE in order for *Experiencing to Be.* Light needed to be, for knowing this and that.
And Light needed Darkness so we could understand the Light....
as well as the Darkness. Darkness is just as pure, as needed as Light.
Darkness is a divine conception, just as Light is.
In darkness, we ponder being and love, family and life.

So our Infinite Being came up with Duality — Father / Mother —
Male / Female, Idea / Expression, Light / Dark, Mind / Breathing
— *Motionless* Ideation .. and Impassioned *Moving* Manifestation.

Infinite Silent Male Mind *C*onceives imagined 'Particles of light'
(within a black emptiness of Infinite restful consciousness).
It conceives of these particles within a 'Shape' of 3 dimensions.
Now Etheric Female Moving-Light-Wave-Essence.. gives direction,
and transportation to the Male Mind generated light 'Particle-Shapes'.
Let us embrace our wholeness in this divine 'Rest and Movement'.
Mind .. and Breath .. Consciousness .. and Motion.
In dark nights we experience meditative rested urge.
Urge moves us forward.
In Light and Urge we activate the motion of Living...
living All the varied aspects of Cosmic Activity.
It is a Movement and Rest — a Motion and Repose.

Often, Photons are thought of as Light. It's not so.
Light is not a particle. *Light is wave-motion,* Photons are "particles"– *(a misunderstood term to begin with)*. Like electrons, protons, etc., they are particles utilized by God, in constructing the universe of things. Yes particles move As – On waves (*a dual masculine–feminine nature of God*) but particles are NOT the wave-motion that they ride on.
We simply cannot measure the indivisible nature of energy *with devices.*
It is way too complex for our measurements.

Light is truly the *invisible waves* that carry All particles to their purpose their shape and form. It is a Current of omnidirectional motion.
Particle ideas come from the Father, and are carried by the Mother.

Throw your hands and arms out from your torso –
that action of directional motion, is more like Light's wave motion.
Light, is like the current in a river, carrying us forward on its powerful irresistible course. Its glides In, On, As, its wave-forms.
Light is the Motion IN and OF the Universe. Light is feminine.
It is the Mother. It is creative Movement.
It creates transportation for all creativity, To and For all construction.

Motionless, Infinite, restful Ideation is Masculine.
The Father Mind is Infinite formless, motionless, creative *Consciousness.*
The planned, designed, experiential origination [in and of all things]
In particles, As particles .. is a masculine architectural function, which resides in absolute clarity of Purpose, Intention, Design and Expression; [and it all happens] within formless invisible, infinite Consciousness.

So our whole Life is a Union of The One and The Other
to experience *in form*, The Many ... AND .. The One...
to Experience Love, Light, Conception-Expression,
Heart and Feelings and Rest and Creativity,
in our light-particled Individual-Body-Form awareness.

This "Union" is a Balancing…
This 'YOGA' = the '*Act of Unification*'
and all of this is for our becoming Greater, than before.

I. Kabala Zohar Yoga

Light is the Motion IN and OF the Universe.
Light is the creative divinely feminine *wave-Movement*. Yet *Motionless, Infinite, Ideation* ..
is divinely masculine.

Before visiting here on the earth-plane,
when we existed in what is currently called a
heavenly *etheric* dimension, we were fully aware
of our Divine-Essence.

I. Kabala Zohar Yoga

In The Beginning...
Spirituality was Before Religion

*I*n ancient times .. human spirituality enjoyed a sublime
Awareness of Oneness, with Divine Being.
This *Awareness of Oneness* sprang from our own Divine-Self awareness.
Before visiting here on the earth-plane, when we existed in what is
currently called a heavenly *etheric* dimension we were fully aware of our
Divine-Essence, and we brought this awareness with us (this powerful
Self expression) when arriving into the uniqueness of this Earth-*living*.

Even passing through the birth canal did not prevent the memory
of our Divinely pure Beingness.
We were born very aware of *Rarefied Being*. We knew that we were
one-with the Infinite life-force-Source of the cosmos.
This ONE is the infinite, Divine invisible Eternal Consciousness.
In our oneness with Divine Being we Also are infinite, invisible
and eternal, but in our Individual expression, as Light Beings,
we manifest our individual self-hood as finite and local beings.

We are in fact a 'Center' of God-Consciousness,
and because God is Eternal, we are too.
But as individual centers of Consciousness we enjoy 'local form,'
enjoying rich and deep experiences which we could not receive *anywhere*
except in this Form of our body-Self-awareness.

It was we ourselves who designed the amazingly beautiful body that
human beings have. We designed it to enjoyably Learn this Life.
In One Square Inch of skin, there are four yards of nerve fibers, 1300
nerve cells, 100 sweat glands, 3 million cells and three yards of blood
vessels. Forty-three pairs of nerves connect the central nervous system
to every part of the body. Twelve pairs go to and from the brain, and
31 nerve-pairings go from the spinal cord. There are nearly 45 miles
of nerves running through our body...to create a sensing masterwork-
masterpiece, for operating in a physical environment.
Our heart beats 40 million times a year, AutoNomically guided by
our brain. Our liver performs 500 different life-preserving functions.

We are of such an *elevated* amazing knowledge and intelligence that designing and genetically implementing our own earth body-form was not only well within our power, but was satisfying as well.

God Inspires and *also* enjoys this designing-manifesting of material energy — for our Form of individuality. *The One* experiences All that we experience. And why would it not be true?   Consider.

It is infinite Divine Mind **giving us** our uniquely *Conscious Portion*.
It is infinite Divine Mind emanating all particles – even for our bodies.
It is infinite Divine Mind that gives a "space" for particles to BE in.
It's infinite Divine Mind that gives them cohesion as Essences.
It's infinite Divine Mind that gives them 'Movement' and a Process for them to do, and experientially perform; (or *motionless inactivity* would rule the scene, with no inherent divine direction).
It is infinite Divine Mind that gives color, speed, direction, texture, purpose and functionality; these aspects cannot arise by themselves. When they exist in Infinite Mind, it is that mind that provides all the 'qualities' of what is held in Its Infinite Awareness. But now, back to us.

We also designed all the animals (*our company here*) and all *insects* and *sea-life* as well. Can you imagine a planet where only plants and humanity existed; with no living creatures to be our company?

So in this distant past we replenished the earth from its previous destructions (from other violences) that were not at-one-with our benevolent heart-nature in our humanity. *Duality* is the rule here. After darkness covered the deep of our local universe and planet (in our *Higher* Form) we replanted, restocked, re-formed, reenergized and reorganized virtually every genetic pattern and molecule of material existence, in this local vicinity of space.

We are the Divine *Elohim*. The uni-plural *Powerful Ones* - oneness. We are the ones who said: "**Let Us make humanity in our image...**" We are The One in the Many, and The Many in the One.

Well, in the back of our minds we knew things would get dramatic, by *playing In* and *Experiencing Duality* and so they have, and so they will. Earth is a temporary experience for us, a sort of fantasy ... island. It is one in a long line of infinite experiences.
The infinitude of environments, universes, dimensions and lives lived in bodies, seem exhilaratingly designed, and wonderfully sublime.

The infinite and creative Mind of God has been and Is eternally capable of bringing us to new exhilaration after new exhilaration. And there is a reason for this motivation in God.

God gets to experience every environment and experience as we do ...With us, In us, As us. We are the divine Uni-plural 'Elohim'. The One in the Many, and the many in the One.

As said our original awareness of oneness preceded all human religion. Religion is one of the poorest ways to feel God. The metaphysics of native indigenous cultures feels Oneness in God more deeply. This prevailing divine awareness in us occurred in the Pre-history of humanity, as we currently think of ourselves.

This awareness was accentuated by the fact that Divine Being is truly Omnipresent and Infinite.
So we therefore knew the *Divine Life, Love, Being* and *Consciousness* were actually located In humanity in our Mind, our Life force, our Breath ... and in our heart full of love and companionship.

Our awareness included the truth that there was not God…**and**…
something else. There is only God — the Great I AM.
We truly understood: "there is only One of us here."
As the first spiritual principle always states: *"In the beginning, God'*
When the Omnipresence of Divine Being is 'individually' realized,
the universe becomes an entirely different 'Place Of Safety,'
to potentially frightened minds. It's is why Psalm 23 says we may

"Walk through the valley of the shadow of death, fearing no evil."
It can be true for the enlightened hearts.
When it is known that Omnipresence is also OmniBenevolence –
– *supportive Love everywhere* – 'Love at the Center of All things'
then the vicissitudes and frightening aspects of reality throughout
the universe…are seen More to be a 'strategy' for enriching our
Soul Awareness, rather than being threats to our Eternal Life.

Since we know, each passing moment and each bit of *knowledge* evolves
and expands our Soul we realize that *increasing awareness* will attend us
throughout our entire life. We even learn from the evil that is expressed.

New *empowering insights* will therefore bless our continuing
consciousness, as a normal state of being, in our *e*ternal Life process.
And the purpose of expressing ourselves 'Locally' – Finitely –
not only serves the enriching purpose for our individual Soul,
but it serves our Infinite Godhead too, who experiences ALL.

So it does not surprise, that ALL of Us, as we pass through new phases, chapters and passages in our experience, can look forward to consistent progress, and a Deepening Enrichment of our Awareness.

One may have guessed by now that our original sublime,
Divine knowledge (*anciently called.. 'Kabala-Zohar Yoga*')…
was either lost, or cast aside in a recurring amnesia in humanity's masses somewhere, in the passages of history.
In *'forgetting our first Estate'* we forgot our original Divine identification; And by losing the most incredible and inspiring Truth of all,
we replaced it with lesser, more painful and damaging religious or governing assumptions. As said, we knew it would get dramatic. Humanity lived by and with these damaging inner assumptions
for most of our "recorded" history.

These lesser assumptions are marked by beliefs that we're on our own in the universe, that, 'we came into the world alone' and will
'leave it alone'. It believes that our life force is <u>not</u> Divine life, but simple human life. Or, some may even believe that Divine Being does not exist. In these 'beliefs' at best, we are separate from God
– believing God is over there, and I am over here.

These assumptions also have Struggle and Limitation as the norm
to our life's growth and progress. These assumptions ironically permeate religious system-beliefs, which should be a place of elevated knowing – and they're in virtually all aspects of human thought as well.
All our spiritual masters, guides, avatars and Messiahs
(most profoundly in the life and love of Jesus)
came into the earthly experience truly Aware – of having a Purpose of uplifting their brother's and sister's 'True Seeing'.
We are here to re-remember our true identity and real purpose.

**"He who knows the All, but does not know himself
has missed everything".** (Jesus, *from "Thomas' Gospel" verse #67*).

**We came into the world unfettered and we will
leave it unfettered.'** (Jesus, *from "Thomas' Gospel" verse #28*).

Wouldn't it be incredible if we made Earth into an Edenic paradise Garden Planet, beyond All comprehension, making it an Oasis of Bliss, for the Souls here, in deepening Harmony?
That's what Jesus and the *Essene message* are bringing to forgetful minds --a Domiciling of Divinity, On Earth. By jolting our *Inner memory with technologies of Transformation*, they show a Path back to our **Oneness-Awareness.** Jesus was raised in the Essene Jewish sect; one of three primary groups. He was not a Pharisee or a Sadducee. The Essene spiritual message goes back to *ancient* days, before Abraham. It was all about our oneness with the *divine Heart and Mind and Breath*. This spirituality is lived in the Now .. of our now-moment awareness.

See, in traversing the lesser painful field of assumptions we learn what real love and true living is Not. And this is actually Good. Understanding the Shadow.. helps us to comprehend the Light. By learning to Let Go the ineffective, inefficient value-belief-systems of the world mind – which our consciousness formerly held to, we begin remembering and reconnecting to the original Truth of 'Kabala Zohar Yoga' – *Oneness with The Splendorous-Light-Within'* in our inner Soul Awareness.

I. Kabala Zohar Yoga

We recapture what we once 'knew' (in another cosmic day)…
but now, we truly Know.
This is the object of all of our lesson-gathering here – to remember our Original Truth "our Creative Power" and our original shared Mind with the Infinite I AM One, while living *HERE*.
This re-cognition of our former 'state' is called an Awakening…
or a re-Awakening-'Shift'.
This is the process many of us are passing through right now…
and it will be so.. in other times and other epochs.

It may now be realized that religion as formed, was a counterfeit curriculum organized by serpentine minds to control the masses *And our money And* our hearts and minds. It keeps us *Away* from our true power and our true nature. It allows elitists in government and religion *to keep us* where they want us – subservient to an ineffective, smothering belief system making them more powerful, and us bridled back into weak self images. And we enter into their empty pursuits – seeking constant diversion, or lazy, unfocused distraction.

Religious structures, environments and teachings more or less *keep us* from advancing *with and into* the Divine Heart. It keeps us right there *with them*…and… *from discovering* our true Soul nature, consciously. By telling us we are wretched sinners, lost in our own darkness, they try to make us the evil ones, when it is *they who are the thieves of Godly love*. Yes, there are also some sweet people there and well intentioned ones but they're spewing dark words, that *they learned* from their teachers… (handed down over millennia). This has been going on a long time.

They want our money or submission…
        'promising' us a freeing-salvation
                that we supposedly don't deserve.

This writing is for making us free – to enter our Divine self-awareness.

So…let this perusing of *"Kabala Zohar Yoga"* [the ancient words]
    (*Oneness with Splendorous-Light-Within*) [the modern words]
be a reconnection and remembering for you… of Your Truth.
For this Truth, will set you Free.

Splendorous Light Within

There's an inner universe within us —
in consciousness —
where The One resides in living Light
with The Other.

II. Present Knowledge

*H*umanity is Divinity in the flesh.
In loving your neighbor you are loving God.
By serving the fatherless, the widow, or helping someone from injury
or trauma, one is serving Divinity. In serving the masses,
we are serving Divinity in her multitudinous forms.
Who would therefore Ever want to steal from God?
Who would ever murder or pillage Divine Being?
Spirituality is not just overlaying a 'template' of civility
or good manners on one's behavior.   No, It Lives.
It is seeing the Divine Everywhere and in everyone,
and rising up in joyfulness that we can serve God —
in each and every face that we see through the day, and
behind the eyes of our beloved, in our child, and even, in our Self.

There's an inner universe within us – in consciousness –
where The One resides in living light with The Other.
This is, from where our unique, individual Soul Self emanates,
including our female and our male energy-aspects.

The One therefore pondered us into being, by expressing us uniquely
apportioning our consciousness and giving us bodies for this universe,
which refine individual awareness – for gathering In salient lessons
in tangible experiential ways, that are 'felt and lived' .. not just known.

The One understands that if we could feel the pain and joys
of 'Life Learning Lessons' in this process here
then .. we'd be truly aware of the inevitable wisdom of Love –
and of love's grace, and its creative joy.
Our Uniqueness imparts individuality here…
And togetherness herein, imparts the graceful wisdom of Love.

Life becomes the true and highest 'partnership of uniting' –
(*our humanity to our Divini*ty) The One in the Many, or the one;
which unification provides us on a continuing basis perfect responses
and inexplicable grace, within our ever-changing realities.

This is a never ending adventure – an eternal play of
Love and Partnership between the Infinite and the Individual.
This is our Bliss.
This is where the Bliss in you comes from, when You feel *God's* Bliss.

How do we facilitate this partnership? We observe the mentation
that fills our mind each moment – any moment – *this moment..* and
replace it with a conversation toward our Inner One, who is our very
consciousness, our very heartbeat, our breath (and the fire in our
"Son-light" sparkle within each of our body's hundred trillion cells.)

We seek insight from The One for how we shall act, think, or speak
for the Highest to continue in our life. We thus pause more.

We go into a mental silence frequently, while listening for a response
from the Still Small Voice.
We become quiet in moment-to-moment doing, *even while conversing,*
sharing, or pondering, and we wait for a blessed Insight
to arrive in awareness, for That moment.
This Listening takes patience while we learn to tune our awareness
to the Leadings of The One. It takes steadfastness as well.
This is a new and everlasting commitment. It is not dropped at the
first, second, or hundredth sign of difficulty.

It's our new life-force .. our new Identity .. our new duty, and our wise
empowerment—in a newly embodied Soul Purpose,
for our newly inspired existence. Read below the Essene view on *Breath.*

****

*"Our Communion is with the Angel of Air; who spreads the perfume of
sweet smelling fields, the rose of Sharon and the spring grass, after the rain.
We* **worship** *the* **Holy Breath** *who is placed Higher than all things created.*
   *For Lo, the eternal and soveriegn luminous space, where rule the
unnumbered stars...***Is the Air we Breathe In and the Air we Breathe Out.**
And in the moment **betwixt** *the breathing in and breathing out is hidden
all the* **Mysteries of the Infinite.** *Angel of Breath* **enter deep** *in me, that I
may know* **All the Secrets** *..."*   adapted from *"***The Gospel of The Essenes***"* –
                                                     by Edward Szekely

Becoming Divinely Human

*I*t is the New You this *Partnership*. You *become* the Divine Human.
It is, *"My Father and I are One .. but my Father is greater than I"* ...
as Christ always indicates. (Our Source-Essence Is The One).

*"The words I speak, and works I DO are Not my own…but they are the
Father Within me... doing the Speaking, and the Working.* 1.

The One individualized As us, is our higher Self. This is called our
Christ-Self. This Christ Self or "Anointed Self" – this Self of pure
Divine Essence and Awareness – is what guides our life's destiny.
The One is where we're being drawn back into, inevitably
for Partnership. When we return our complete awareness to this Source,
we've reached the highest mark, the highest most sublime state of being
in our Universal experience.

> *"He who knows the All, but does not know The Self,
> has missed everything."* 2.

In knowing our true SELF we shall be in dominion over The All.

*'Now there's neither Jew nor Greek, slave nor free, nor male or female –
for now, it is just 'Christ'* (**the Royal Anointed One**) *– All in All'.* 3.

You see, this dedication of being 'partnered to our Christ Being-ness'
will be part of our life, forever.
It began in true earnest on planet Earth about 2000 years ago.
The blessed milestones we pass on the way are so exhilarating, and the
passages of this our journey of true spirituality, are so blissfully fulfilling,
that we'll never give up this partnership. The interior romance with our
Higher Self .. And its ebulliently satisfying ways, gives us
stratospheric pleasure in Consciousness. We're never alone.

When we realize WHO walks with us through every stride…
we will not fear, and divine Love may be felt in every step.

Splendorous Light Within

The Eyes of Love, Need, Insight,
Desire, and Attentive Awareness are Alive, and
Breathing in Animals.

Divine Mind Shines in 'Everything'

*J*ust as God is the life, breath and consciousness in each of us,
The One is also the life-force intelligence in animals.
It is Divine Being behind the eyes of all creatures.
The idea of instinct in creatures was a concept postulated only *recently*
when people could not explain the intuitional patterns and inherent
awareness in their animals. They 'question' Divine Soul Awareness
in animals. The eyes of love, insight, maternal desire and attentive
awareness are *Alive and Replete* in animals. Don't be deceived.
They love, bathe, Parent, play, have Intent, shyness, build, fear, doubt,
anger, hunger, thirst, sorrow, sleep, dream, and .. *they* **die with a sigh.**

The Divine life-force intelligence operates through the animal's DNA
creating the inimitable characteristics and 'nature' of each creature.
It is *The One* nonetheless infusing those muscles with abundant energy
or craftily being the qualities of each creature in charm and humor,
or domestic love and service in our company, or the raw power
and ferocity of beasts in the jungle deep, or under the sea.

This is one way The One teaches us <u>and</u> participates in our universe.
Earth is our recreational "theme park," zoo, fantasy island, and school
ground. The mind of *The One* maintains all Reality for and in all of us.

> '*The Earth delights to <u>feel</u> your bare feet and the winds
> long to play with your hair.*' 4.

In the outer universes we appear to live in light, so we may experience
that environment – and it Is true, we do experience 'particles' of light
in the outer universe; but they are not the eternal Infinite Light *within*
each of us (*our Divine selfhood*).

These temporary particles of light are needed to give us our
experiential awareness of the things .. events .. and beings
of this physical universe, within our Consciousness.

"Let there be Light" was spoken so we could experience the *outer,*
visible universe…(not our Inner universe).

Light always existed within *The One* as pure conscious awareness of Being, as I AM-ness here, now. Light is the moving intelligence. The One Self ponders. *Ponders Stability.* Infinity and emptiness are similar. Motion and Rest stabilize the ALL, in an essence of 'Mystery-Balance'. After becoming involved with the outer universe, fascinated and even occasionally addicted to it — as individualities are known to do herein — we actually become Less interested in satisfying our minds and hearts with the things of the outer universe. This is good.

This is the lesson we are learning in the material universe.
After experiencing the outer to certain degrees of satiation
we will inevitably tire over it, and we will look within again for
our True satisfaction – uniting again consciously in Partnership..
with The One.
After we've had our time of independence and wayward journeying,
we will realize the bliss of partnership with The One,
who provides us literally everything .. forever and ever.

The One has great admiration and gratitude for all who live here
in this 'dualistic' universe. Angels and other orders of spirit beings
Divinely powerful Archons, Cosmic and galactic Spirits are always
with and in Concert with The One.
But the revered status as "Child of God" belongs to humanity. Why?
Because living in Time and three dimensions,
is a great and challenging trial.

When the infinite motionless Male Mind of *The One* united with the Divine Feminine moving Essence of Creative Intelligence, giving us birth as Divine Children – we got both Male and Female aspects of our Divine Progenitors, from their Being and we were Whole in our selves. So this revered status as Local Divine Beings, was engendered by God.

But on Earth, there's a searing wisdom from almost infinite friction by being enclosed in the flesh — subjected to gravity, heat and cold, violence, starvation, broken bones, sickness, disease, victory and valor, along with Parenthood, in birthing family.
Then there's the enervating endless chain of Cause and Effect realities constantly hovering over us.

And finally some unknown and fearful Death ends our life on earth.
Well .. the Angels behold and stare in silent amazement…
But they do not really understand the trials of our lives.

Please know and appreciate that just being Born on our planet
is an unfathomable Experience and challenge particularly when
it is a Spirit-Soul of Bliss, who is arriving here into the experience.
I say to you, that souls who live, *just a few short years in the flesh,*
before passing on from accident or illness, have moved *'mountains'*
of Awareness Into their consciousness, regarding this experience.
They've added immensely to their *fund of knowledge* of True Loving
…and empathetic compassion.

Our willingness, to allow our selves and our Souls to experience such
extremes of life and livingness is incomprehensibly valued, favored,
and admired by The One. *You* are a Treasure for being here.

When Divine Being imagined the entirety of the universes and all that
they included through eternity, He knew this universal stage would
have to be populated in order for the cosmic story to be enacted.
After imagining the universal story The One desired to <u>live</u> it.
Being the Alpha and Omega already, *The One* desired to experience
the "in-between" as well.

All the talents in each of us are Divine Qualities…*beautiful* expressions.
You see, it is God who is the Life in all of us – our consciousness,
our senses, our breath, the mind-generated *'particled body-form',*
as well as the loving empathic sentience in each of our hearts.

He can never leave us or forsake us. She will always be with us,
to the end. God wouldn't ask us to Do something He-She wouldn't do.
The One is ONE with us — as our life-force and consciousness.
Remember always: 'There's only one of us here.'

From Bliss … Into The Earth

She knew, that the souls who passed through to <u>live</u> the Divine Story
and its Plan would be the finest, most mature, refined creative,

disciplined and tender-loving beings She'd ever emanated.
And at the conclusion of their journey, that…they would in fact
be smaller Selves of the Divine I AM .. or .. 'Local' DIVINE Beings.
They already ARE the divine 'Elohim' -- the plural divine *Ones,*
within The Infinite One.
The Infinite One will always be The One who inhabits eternity
and infinity, but these, these Children of God, these children
of the Universe … would be God in a 'local' finite realm.

When we all lived in the realm of Spirit-Bliss how could we FEEL the
wisdom of charity and harmony? – the salience of absolute tenderness?
In fact, in that other realm, we knew nothing BUT the grace
of a Divinely ordered universe. "Up there" is pure bliss and fullness.
We could not possibly understand the grace of sharing, of modesty,
of self-control and discipline, or of Self-Sacrifice and Sorrow.

When we LIVE in bliss and carefree Exploration of infinite byways
where <u>all</u> is provided, thirst and hunger are inexplicable concepts to us.
How could we possibly understand the 'Deep' of loving, or of kindness?
How could we possibly understand the feeling of seeing our baby cry, or
suffer? How could we possibly understand the verities and vicissitudes
of Striving – or the salient pain of Loss?

The longer we stay and endeavor in the outer universe, the more
inevitably drawn to and intuned to our inner Light we will become.
It is living 'the circle'. This is as it should be. We are learning in all
things to separate the wheat from the chaff. We always return to bliss.

"*This Light is the true Light, that lights everyone…
who comes into the world*". 5.

This is where we come from, and it is our Heading…
this *Kabala-Splendor of Conscious Inner Light.*
Regarding our stultifying ego life, we spend much time
pondering 'the Past' of our life.
But we are to neutralize that habit by daily practicing a 'Yoga'
(or a 'Unification') by partnering our Inner to our Outer awareness.
Let the Inner Self guide and love the outer selfhood.

We must <u>ever</u> be about this process. It is an act of Love toward the Inner One, and toward our self. It is not an act of will, but an endeavor of our heart. It is fed with the energy of enthusiasm and exuberance, which come from our heart. With these energetic attitudes 'in play' we can make transcendent leaps in progress in the now moment of our current life experience. It is these two magical energies from Divine Being within, that will transform any or all of the matters of "self" that burden awareness.

The One also adds to our strength when we have impassioned yearning for The One leaving behind Ego (with enthusiasm and exuberance). This means we leave behind the Past of our life's down-pulling memories (its dualistic pains and value-judgments of limitation).

NOTE: Have you ever wondered *why* atheists feel so strongly about the nonexistence of God? My book *Breath of Light* covers it thoroughly. But here's a note on Michelangelo, and Roman toenails.
The reason so many atheists or agnostics have a problem with GOD is they cannot see beyond the white haired god with toenails on the ceiling of the Sistine Chapel.
The Romans made God with toenails and elbows .. and white hair.

The Jewish faith had an *Infinite One* – an invisible consciousness permeating time-space and eternity (i.e. an infinite Consciousness **manifesting As its ideas**). God is *not* A being .. GOD .. **IS Being.**

Each of us has to see that the Cosmos comes from 'Being' – not nothing. All things in existence come *from Being,* Not non-being. This is the problem with evolutionists – they believe everything started from *nothing or NON-Being.* It's illogical and indicates mental *shallowness.* When anyone is awed by the incredible size of the cosmos, thinking a white haired older gentleman, sitting on a marble chair made it all, it stretches mental credulity. That's why they argue so vehemently. Once we share that infinite formless **Beingness** expresses its ideas, they may finally see it .. that **Beingness** designs and expresses All things. They already DO believe in **beingness, and intelligence ..** Theirs, Ours, and in everything and everyone .. now they just have to see it in the *Macroscopic Cosmos* too.

Splendorous Light Within

Fullness in our earth life, from it's beginning to the present, includes up and down, back and forth, rich and poor... joy and sorrow... birth and death — all of the dualities of life, within matter-energy.

III - The Pain of 'Me' Leads Us to Our Divine Partnership

Our 'apparent' selfhood out here in the world, is just a particle
of who we are – a mere shadow of Us, that is operating herein.
We identify with this apparent selfhood because it appears in a
continuum of experiences called 'Me'.
This string of Me experiences is unique and enclosed in our individual
awareness and is unique from everyone else's 'Me' experiences.
We've always had a string of Me experiences that are unique to us.
Our perspectives, on living and experiential reality, are all ours,
and are unique from everyone's.
We identify AS this Me identity here now,
because we have experienced its continuum of awareness.
Prior, we have had many other Me moments too.

We Feel all the pains and joys that this 'continuum of awareness'
passes through.
We identified with the victories and were saddened by the losses.
This is how this system teaches us lessons.
God's pre-Destined story, which we live, makes
"*hearts Sweet with hunger and with thirst*". 6.

This tendering and endearing of Awareness expands personal
responsibility and responsiveness. It enlarges our heart with compassion.
The sad times and losses create beautiful Soul compassion In us.
We cannot grow fully in our totality without the darkness of sorrow
and doubt. A one sided being has only one side.

Fullness includes up and down, back and forth, rich and poor,
inner and outer, rehearsal and performance, doing and watching,
joy and sorrow, birth and death – all of the dualities of life, et. al.

Yes, the joys are ecstatic, and laughter is a most marvelous gift from
The One... and what would life be without the loving embrace of our
Beloved's arms and breath, cascading across our shoulders or neck...

but the sadness and compassion that human experiences engender,
make us Rich, in our hearts. Rich hearts make us generous.
We become quality Soul Expressions.
So as we live day-to-day we must partner <u>each</u> moment with The One
to consciously Partner our <u>Inner</u> TO the outer 'Me'- Selfhood
(uniting the Divine within, to our daily actions and responses).
This continual focus on Partnership with our Divinity within
then becomes the ever-present endeavor of our life.

Thus, the all-encompassing bless'ed dream, becomes the reality
of our life's purpose. Think.
If you were supposed to remember 'something' ALWAYS and ever
on an every minute basis, how Easy it would become to Practice it
moment to moment; because it is the One thing that
you have centered ALL your activities on.

You would not do anything outside the Light of this over-riding
construct, because you'd Weave it into the very fabric of your life's
every-awareness and every Event.

It becomes the One objective in your being.
This, my friends, is the 'Christ Consciousness' state of Being…
and it is our very purpose, in our individualization.

Being CONSCIOUSLY One-With The Divine One Within You
is the purpose here, when in a dualistic world reality.
We are each equally the male Mind and the feminine Breath essence
of the Divine Father - Mother.

When The One and The Other united to express individualities like us,
at the inception of all, we received *each half* of 'Them' AS us…
we received *Wholeness* .. as Complete Divine Ones.

And a wonderful truth we may glory in, is that we are One-With
the infinite Divine Mind when we are back up there; yet we know
the uniqueness of our past 'ME' identities holographically "backward"
 – giving us a unique perspective on all of LIFE, as we Experienced

III. The Pain of 'Me'

Our continuum of awareness. Down here though we submit ourselves purposely to an Amnesia of our Divine Identity, to make this real for us.

Now then, we shall always be Conversing with our Divine Father–Mother within .. in moment-to-moment camaraderie. When the 'sense' of separation from Divine Being finally ceases, Life is pure grace.

When once we've tasted the beauty of this romantic Spiritual bliss … with our Inner Selfhood, being 'ego-drawn' will be a thing of the past. We may face challenges along the way – and yes, even pains, but those… are merely the salient verities and vicissitudes of life in this world, which are Here to enrich our hearts and our consciousness.

Splendorous Light Within

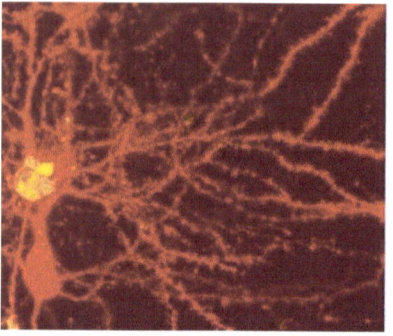
Energy Pattern in the Human Brain

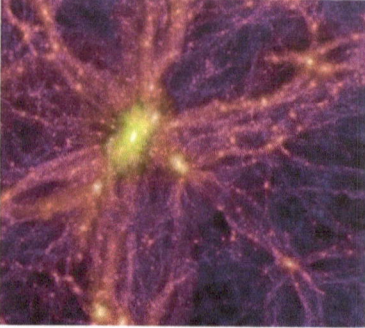
Energy Strands In the Universe

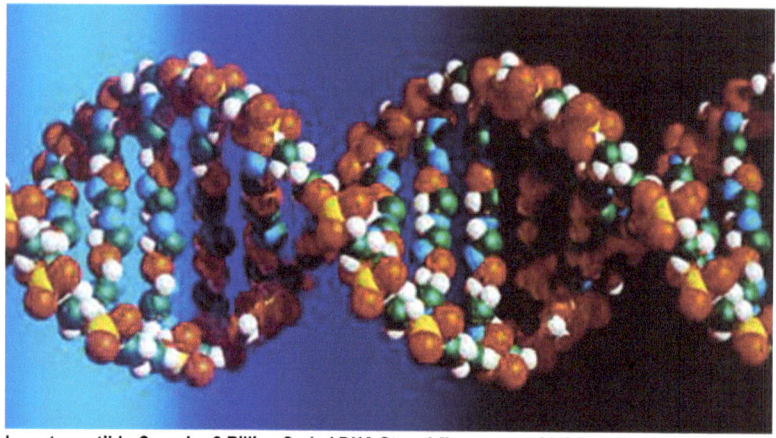
Incontrovertibly *Complex* 3 Billion Coded DNA Strand *[Language of Life]*

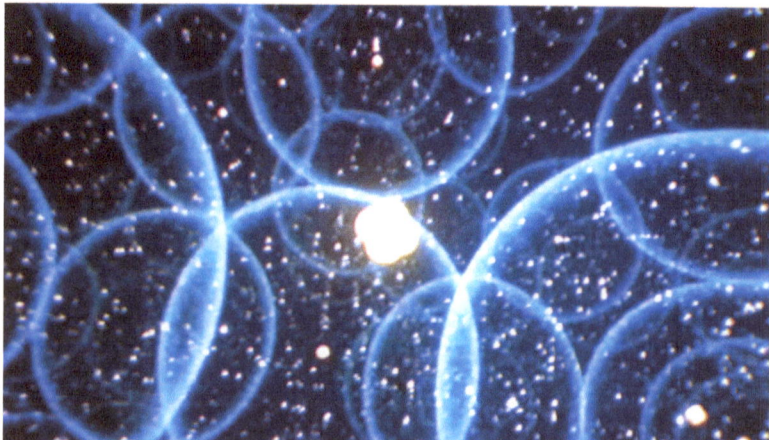
The Energy of Life and SPACE is Mostly Emptiness, with Whirling Vortices of Light – *a Puzzle* – Baffling Scientists for Over a Century. With emptiness, how does "shape" come to BE?

IV - The Dimension of Infinite Mind Binds Everything Together

When it is understood there is a Dimension above the physical universe (undetectable to scientists and devices, as it's not Part of this Universe) one will realize that God is truly the Idea Creator Initiator-Sustainer of all realities in the universe (of literally every particle-construct in the universe and beyond). This is all conceived and "particle-expressed" in Divine mind, which holds all things together.
Just as we understand the *rules of a game* we are playing while we play it, God's mind endlessly 'Adheres' all things within their structures. If you do not think Divine Mind expresses every energy particle and molecular pattern, then what "intelligent-emotive-impulse" of manifestation does give it expression? And What provides the cohesion to the atomic 'partner-entities' (seen in such as the *electrons, protons and neutrons*) in remaining subatomically together, as essences?

In the image down to the left WHY do those particles "hang together"? If Divine Mind is not giving-emanating birth to these vortexes of "particle" – energy, *What is?* And HOW would cohesive assemblage occur for every cosmic element, as the wondrous *molecules, compounds, and materials* giving expression to our entire cosmos--*Darwin's dumbluck* in haphazard accidents?? Sorry. It can not be. Why is it anyway, *dumbluck accidents* are the atheistic explanations for beauty?
Why should dumbluck be an origin to Infinite Lawful Order?

To believe in a Void of matter-energy [*where all supposedly started in an empty accident of Nothingness*] and then claim that matter-energy simply sprang into existence – with no cause or SOURCE for it's inherent sublime diversity [not to mention it's very existence] is to brush away the principle of Causation, and to say Effects come into existence with no source. Who'd postulate such a silly idea? About 95% of humanity believes in Divine Intelligence. Darwin and his students believe in accidents. Truly. They believe in no cause. It's all dumbluck. Why? Because giving credit to principle means something *like God* exists.

When a mother says to her child '*Who made the mess in this room'?* The child knows its cause.

When seeing a car we know a car company made it.
When seeing Encyclopedias we know vast numbers of people
stood on each other's shoulders over centuries, to cause its existence.
When seeing Mt. Rushmore we know a sculptor worked years on it.

So to say that Nothing gave cause or expression to what's an amazing infinitude of designs and perfect harmonious principles
(within Incomprehensible Inter-Activity) among universal Laws (which are Invisible, constant, Perfect and Unassailably Infinite) and without whose guiding invisible constructs nothing would ever be initiated or maintained, is just pure silliness. Nothing would ever come together, or lawfully hold together – never. Infinite Laws are crucial.

Darwinists say quadrillions of Accidents gave expression to an infinite number of energies, particles, atoms, molecules, vapor, compounds, elements, fractal designs, materials, solids, liquids gases, galaxies, radiation, nebula, stars, lightspeed, black holes, rotation, revolutions, circles, spheres, squares, triangles, awesome Fibonacci sequences 'everywhere,' gravity, atomic force-ratios, space, vibration, geometry, planets, oceans, dirt, mountains, heat, fresh water, hot, cold, ice, snow, photosynthesis, chlorophyll, nourishment, fruit, nutrients, vitamins as well as Ova and Spermatazoa…uterine walls, umbilical cords, placentas, birth..Nurturing mothers, mother's breast milk, suckling babies? And all this comes through an Infinitude of 'Dumb-Luck' accidents? Nope.

And how did the exact Same system of phallus, Sperm, Ova and Womb (seeding, gestation, birthing) come to be in All species?
It has to work the first time incidentally (in both sexes at once) or there's no species [nor any continuity of Species]. Understand.. continuity is the bugaboo for atheists. For a Continuity of Species to BE the procreative system must be perfect the first time in the first opportunity, in the fortunate mutated creature or there's no species. See, mutational evolutionary changes truly take hundreds or thousands of years between mutations. If an "almost perfect" creature for procreating is missing just One aspect of the birthing system (*i.e. no fallopian tubes*) a creature would die long before the next mutation even occurs.
Suggesting that a whole *system* could come **in a single mutation** is silly.
It doesn't happen now, why would it happen then?

IV. Infinite Mind Binds Everything

Mutations are not creative – just an 'affective' occurrence. It is like *changing* one *digit* in a binary computer code. Some thing is going to be different *but what?* So, WHY is it ALWAYS turning out so beautifully for a universe to be and *quadrillions* of amazing life forms being *perfectly expressed?* So we could only hope that the next mutation was about adding these missing fallopian tubes. What if the next mutation was about fingernails happening not in them but a creature 90 miles away? We may now see, that dumb-luck-accidents are not a reliable form of change for species continuity to Be, because partially mutated creatures die too quickly...before they're complete. This is what evolutionary folks never address. Why should evolutionary changes keep improving the Same Entity ...who is "Almost Ready" in that One life? Death occurs too fast. Their theory doesn't even address this. Listen closely.

How could sexual Procreative Apparati come into existence for any species (let alone All) in BOTH sexes simultaneously as an "Accident" turning Out Perfectly the first Time (for Every species everywhere)? It requires perfection in every accident. This is their theory. They say the phallus and the vagina were "Symmetrical accidents" unfolding in billions of species ongoingly – mammals, fish, insects, birds. How? Why? Why's it always the *'Same Design' in all Accidents?* Mathematicians giving us the odds of this happening simultaneously in just One species (*creating both male and female that fit each other at once*) is preposterously astronomical (let alone in every species on a planet or in the cosmos).

If one doesn't have the complete procreative system in place the first time – happening in 2 different entities who are Next to each other in time-space (who also need an Interest in Sexual coupling) they must Know 'How' to implement the sexual act (with no prior experience). They must have a desire toward it, then succeed at seeding that womb with Ova and sperm working perfectly in that very First attempt [this has to be true in all Species on Earth, or a continuity for that or any species will never occur]. Without simultaneously perfect mutational sexual accidents, we'd never have any species nor *infinite variety* in living creatures. And how did the sperm accidentally arise and have a phallus to **send it**; or how did the ova arise and have a uterus and fallopian tube *already there*, for creation to work...being in BOTH sexes accidentally at once...*in every species everywhere?* No one ever asks how a tiny Hormone (made of several 'light-particle-atomic-structures') has the compelling power to reveal sexual hunger, vitamin deficiencies or ambition. *WHO* tells Adrenaline to make us exert Massive Instant Action to escape trouble? .. *who, how, why?* Why is it that smart? The procreative Apparatus in a species HAS To Be perfect in a male and a female Simultaneously (they both need a mutational accident, making them Male and Female respectively at the same moment with ALL the systems for Procreation Perfect *right then*) all at once or that species will never exist. And here's the final consternation for *atheistic believers.* WHERE did any Species come from anyway .. if no *operating procreative apparatus* existed prior? Friends, truly, they'd never even BE here for mutational sexual accidents to occur within − if there was no procreative apparatus or ability beforehand. They *must* be birthed.

So let us discuss the Domain of this conscious dimension *Above* the known Universe, which is best be described as a place of Mind, and mind-forms. For its 'Thought-Form' projected Structures are what atomic and subatomic particles Adhere To to maintain the form, shape and reality of all material essences in existence, every where. Ask yourself, what Causes perfectly Independent quantum particles, floating here and there, to form into molecules, then, adherently *attach* into material forms called Material Reality.. and How, Why, do they find and adhere to each other so harmoniously when they are floating around, then somehow 'decide' to become miraculous structures such as Carbon, Nitrogen or Uranium? And where does the awesome energetic *Radiation* in Uranium, come from? And why not from *all* vortices?

Scientists cannot say Why there are 92+ elements in the universe, having distinct structures from all others. They know that there are differing 'substance-structures' in the universe, they just don't know what Causes these differing structures to be held in place, as distinct from the others. However, we know *something Invisible* provides a 'Form' which holds all the protons, electrons, quarks and muons in place, as well as the potential vibrational strings at their foundation. It provides the basis to *assemble all substances.* It's a thought-form projected from above and around the universe *holographically* and it maintains the universe while it maintains all physical realities for *everything* in its borders. Today it's called dark matter-dark energy — an essence of *'something'* that is described as *Nothing,* giving form to the somethingness all over. It gives Shape and Volume to all things. It's what **Kirlian Photography** reveals – an invisible structure within it all. Seeing those photos, of the Kirlian ghost-shapes, is truly amazing to us.

Now Consider our DNA—that IT is held in place also, similarly to atomic structures. We know that DNA is the Map and rule of law that creates the qualities and characteristics In and Of all living things – one-cell life, amoeba, plankton, algae, plant-life, insects, animals, human beings, sea creatures, and all living things anywhere. The color, bone structure, size, ferocity, life-length, leaves, skin, bark, tendons, nerves, brain, talents, amiability, and total seen and unseen nature of all Living things, is guided and informed in its essence by its DNA.

DNA is the 3-billion-coded-strand <u>Program</u> that Life operates from and whose informational rules it all adheres to. Atheistic believers have no explanation for how something millions of times more complex than a Super-Computer just stumbled into being, in simple dumb-luck. They've no explanation if anyone is asking.
It's the most insurmountable aspect of their theory.
They say everything came into being through "dumb-luck".
Can you believe folks who say **all things** sprang into being by accidents? Nothing *congeals magically* today, why would it occur then? DNA is so complicated.. mathematicians say that it can never happen accidentally or *stumble into being* by chance. They have *super-computers* calculating the odds of every permutation of this being able to happen. Sorry.
No Accident can just 'congeal' 3 billion ordered codes .. producing Glorious Life.

So now ask your self (*because they'll never tell you*) how could something infinitely *more complex than a computer* simply stumble into being? What forces would compile-construct it, with its insightful assemblage, with codes directing the formation of organs, ears, eyes, stomach, liver, lungs, brains-hearts beating *72 times* a minute *(with brain directing it)*? **How did mutations occur in every species telling all brains to beat all hearts with electricity, rhythmically? Where did the 'rhythm' come from?**

Our DNA strand is an actual language, with an *alphabet, grammar-rules* and ordered proper formats; and if we looked within it, we might even find the code structure in its very construction.

Now, why did WE invent language so long ago?   Well, so we could tell each other things – *information on fishing or hunting*. See, languages are vehicles for information. A blood vessel is not the blood itself, but it carries and delivers the blood. The delivery system delivers the thing. Languages deliver information. See DNA is replete with/as information. HAVING language and sharing information requires, and indicates *[beyond the shadow of a doubt]* that 'Consciousness' is present between parties. One talks the other listens. Friends, our cells talk to each other. Oh my. Cells have Consciousness? Yes. See the You-Tube video below.

In his book, Darwin offered a caveat to his theory, essentially saying that if it could ever be proven that multitudinous systems required each other to exist and survive forward so that the systems would have to arise 'fully assembled simultaneously' (*impossible by his own admission*) then his theory would be proven wrong. This is Darwin's admission not ours. Darwin's followers do not wish anyone to know this comment. If people knew he actually wrote that, they'd think again about evolutionary theory. When people's paychecks are at risk, they stay silent. Well we're there now. There are so many systems within all life forms, even within every cell, which require each other to live that they would have to have arisen simultaneously for everything to survive.

Darwin thought cells were filled with a *jelly-like fluid*. Actually there are myriad Mechanisms of untold amazing designs in awe-inspiring details ... of structure and purpose. And they need each other every moment of existence, and cannot survive forward without the other systems present in the cell. Darwin believed the cell mutated into a perfect existence in mere seconds. And if it was not a few seconds, it would have died immediately. All those mechanisms and systems need to be there.. for the whole cellular system to live.   See that video across, at its URL.

But what is really in our cells if not Darwin's assumed 'jelly'?
It's just amazing. There are actual platforms to which other objects are fastened for stability. Really. That means "fastener" mutations would have to occur, for them to arise to existence. There are also Membranes *[see Pic on the page across]* which separates things, like walls.

IV. Infinite Mind Binds Everything

Notice in these 5 left side images the myriad details of construction and function. Darwin suggested these cell structures arose by 'Accident' in mere seconds. We now know the cell's millions of systems 'need each other' to survive forward each moment. They could not have arisen in stages – only ALL at once. Divine design is its author.

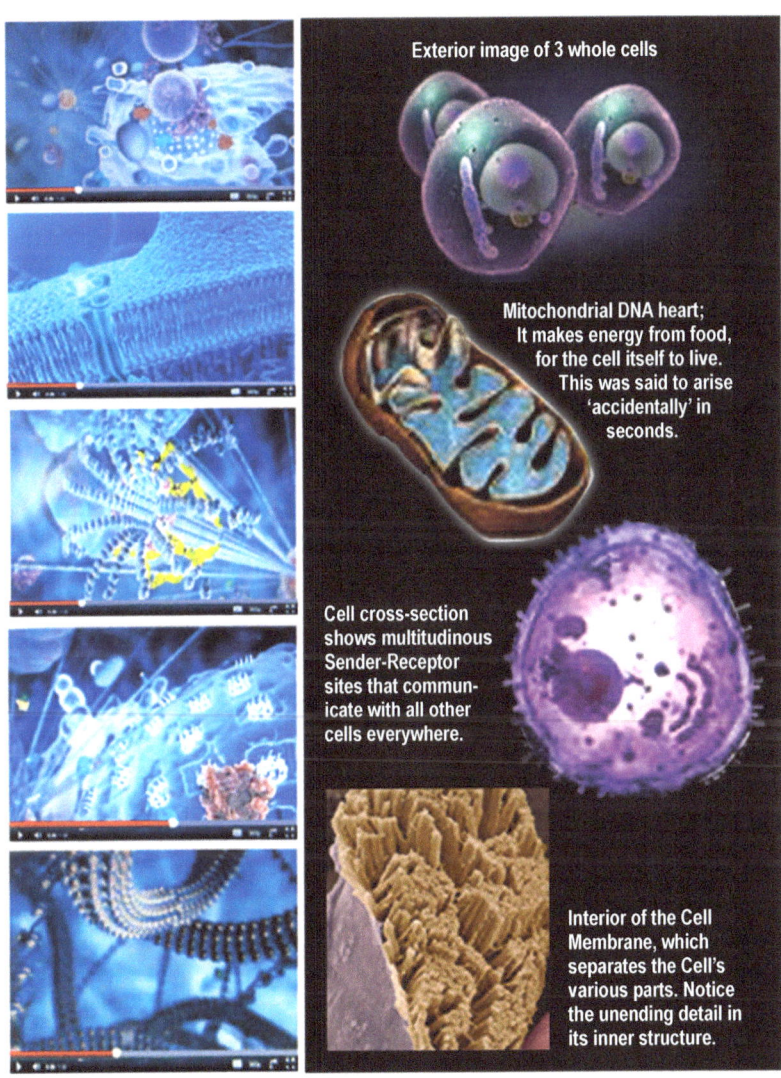

Exterior image of 3 whole cells

Mitochondrial DNA heart; It makes energy from food, for the cell itself to live. This was said to arise 'accidentally' in seconds.

Cell cross-section shows multitudinous Sender-Receptor sites that communicate with all other cells everywhere.

Interior of the Cell Membrane, which separates the Cell's various parts. Notice the unending detail in its inner structure.

To view the above You-Tube Animation Showing the Cell's Complexity,
Go to: http://youtu.be/ZDH8sWiUsAM (Link to You-Tube Cell Animation)

There are also tubes shooting protein streams. **Millions** of *electrical sender-receptors* also exist, that send 'information' to other cells.
There are also *Factories* that make amino acids and proteins.
There are also many other *Structures* (many mutations).
There's a spinning propeller (*Flagellum*) whirling at 10,000 rpm that can stop in an instant, and spin the other direction. That's a complicated system and it was all suppose to congeal in a few seconds, in very good luck, into a very intelligent design, through a single mutation. Darwin actually thought this. Come on. *Millions* of systems in one mutation? Sorry.
Get real. Could all the systems arise at once, with a single dumb-luck tweaking? Could a mutation command the arrangement of quadrillions of molecules into many perfect substances, shapes, relationships (tubes, walls, electrical receptors, propellers, factories) all electrically talking? Darwin didn't even know they communicated. The Darwinians today don't understand that either. Why? Their theory can't answer it.

Just as a house is made of wood, concrete, metal, carpet, plastic, so is the cell made of many different essences or materials. Could those many esoteric decisions be made by a single mutation? Could a mutation *form* a propeller that's required for the whole system to work *inside*, with *moving fluid streams* (by commanding atoms from the Ether into the shape of a propeller?) No. With no flagellum the Cell dies – it needs that propeller creating motion within the cell! We need motion all over.

Since all development is a random accident, as *They say*, HOW is it that gyroscopic balancing mechanisms are present in the Ear and Brain in virtually all living things? *Gyroscopes keep fighter jets aloft*. They keep all of us in physical balance – not tripping, falling down. Not nauseous. Are we to believe an accident of amazing Gyroscopic Inner Science happened billions of times, randomly, in all creatures? Now consider this; if a projected-thought-form from the DEEP of Divine-Mind creates and maintains all essences and atomic forms—whether animate or inanimate—then the DNA map in all living things is not a random or accidental occurrence of creation (which somehow stumbled into being). No it's held in place by a divine thought-form structure- 'Decision' to Be…just what it is deeply in the DNA's structured intelligence. In other words DNA is also purposefully sent forth into existence by the thought form projections of Divine-Mind, not only at its inception but throughout its existence. This includes the DNA of genetic disabilities, and inherited predispositions, defects, talents, gifts, athleticism also the intelligence, in You and everyone – even in all creatures and *plants*. This means hereditary abilities and disabilities are Divinely designed and maintained by *The One* for our 'partnered' Use.

The great I AM of Infinite-Eternity has selected Each and every thing for-Being-In-Existence in its unique essence – including You and your DNA. Since You ARE This One, You're *being You* on purpose. Because divine mind (expressing the Universe) is the author of all science and composition, how can anything be outside of God's conscious plan? Why wouldn't this be true, by the way?
Why wouldn't an Infinitely Aware, Infinitely Creative Being (*whose consciousness, essence and Intention inhabits all energy and material reality*) also know That and How every essence Is, just what it is?
Each is expressed by the Divine One and is maintained in its structural existence as well, every moment, by that Mind, *holding* everything.

DNA is not just the language of life that is irresistibly complex and puzzling, but one has to ask, how something the size of a few atoms can contain, and is ABLE to Impart the musical genius of Mozart, the Art of Da Vinci, or design a tiger's face? How and why do quantum particles have Art ability inside them? How does a particle command vision and eyeballs and in all creatures. How could a particle be smart? It is only in God's mind-plan that a particle can have a Divine Intention in it. The existence of every physical life-form in the universe has their DNA as a veritable 'god' which delineates and sends forth the life-form in all uniqueness into interaction, with all other aspects and beings of creation. Now.. here is one of the most damning and irrefutable *Disproofs* against evolution. **Sameness** in almost all creatures is Not mathematically possible. A "too present feature" like miraculous eyeballs with lids, lenses, retinas, aqueous humor, in *every species* is not random!

Realize. Human beings are *"sleepy"* unaware beings (in the diminished state that we inhabit). We are having a sleepy unaware experience on purpose. We get to say "**So this is what that feels like**."
This reality and this system are set-up this way for our conscious use.

As a Divine Being *up there* we are complete, mature, open, and yet ready for our rich and meaningful experiences of human sharing and growingness. Yet here, we cannot see right in front of us, the reality of a situation staring us in the face with our current capabilities. Otherwise *How* would divine light beings get to *Have this experience* of *diminished states* or stumbling capacities? Our natural state is divine wholeness, omniscience – Lighted Being. Our psyches here, are delicate and fragile so the fury of ego-hood is deemed to be strength (*from an unenlightened perspective*). We often have habitual suspicion here that some are out to get, deceive or misdirect is, but we often don't know, until hindsight's arrival what the facts are. Human nature is deeply involved in simple hope and fear (it's just weakness). But we are having this 'me' identifying *self-experience* purposely, to enrich our Souls with an experience of weakness, compassion, empathy. You chose to be here as You purposely. Go ahead, own it, Own You. You're the Progenitor of your experiential richness and expansion. You're here to BE you.

If We Do Not See Divine Brilliance Everywhere We Do Not Really See

We are so connected to our body-Identity, we miss out on the magic of Divine Consciousness.. everywhere.. *even In Us.*
Our senses are tuned so *low* they don't perceive the scientific realities of the quantum world (the basis of our 3 dimensional cosmos).
The 'tuning' of our visual cortex is incredibly narrow. We miss out on what's occurring among all the other light-wave-lengths which we can not perceive. Since we cannot see subatomic particles we are ignorant of their reality, their movement and trajectory. We do not see the *underneath* of the universe (the place of Divine Mind) which gives birth to ALL of this. We cannot see the interior tapestry of Time and Space. We cannot see the *molecular roadway* beneath the *paved road.*
We do not perceive our etheric body, inside our corporeal form.
We're not aware of all the filament-like connections or causative web of past and future realities, enclosing our Present moment.
We tend to live here like our life occurs in a theme-park, where all the experiences are "set-up" for the ticket-buyer.
We *feel* our past; we cannot *see* the future, so we must finally focus on the present, to remove the influence of past pains.

IV. Infinite Mind Binds Everything

DNA is able to Impart the
musical genius of Mozart, the Art of Da Vinci,
or design a tiger's face.

Most people feel the universe is a separate, neutral, objective place and they are inescapably IN it. Things are solid, space is empty, Fire is hot, water's wet, life is fragile, laughter is wonderful, Love is warm, and children are beautiful. And if they ever even consider quantum subatomic realities, they see it as a place of indescribable energy that apparently 'runs itself' automatically, silently and some how perfectly. They don't think of it as being 'run' or coordinated consciously by God in a divinely-determined 'organizing' of the Divine. No they see it some how being inertly, effortlessly there, and just 'what is'. But the truth is, the over arching, completely prevalent interpenetrating and permeating nature of Divine Mind actually creates <u>every</u> *subatomic particle* throughout infinity (*influences their path to molecular construction*) and organizes energetic and material reality for all essences every where, including all life forms (their instinct and their actions, and intelligence).

We are each expressed by Divine Mind in the Divine plan, with the objects we work with, and matters with which we deal, the emotional ones, the logical ones, the sweet ones and yes, even the painful ones.

Did you ever wonder: *How much influence and direction in My life comes from God?* How much of your life and being do You see, as simple randomness, or as a conscious plan of Divine Being?

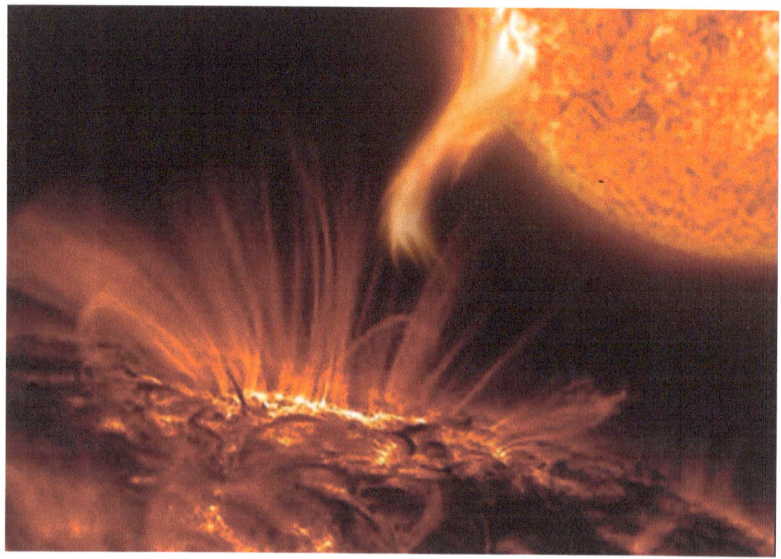

IV. Infinite Mind Binds Everything

Your life and DNA is <u>not</u> an accidental happenstance of the cosmos that just happened to fall in place. Predestination is the ancient truth-teaching that the Essenes famously taught, that Christ and Paul also taught in their teaching (that God has given birth to the entirety of the cosmic story). This is why prophets can Prophesy. The word *Predestination* is mentioned about a half dozen times in the Bible. Why? We may now understand the verse in Isaiah "***God calls the End from the Beginning.***" And the verse in Revelation: "***The Lamb was slain from the foundations of the world.***" Then there is Isaiah 45 [a consternation to theologians for a very long time].

"I form the light and I create darkness: I make peace and I create evil. I the Lord do all things. Shall the clay say to the Potter:"What are you making?"

Let it be said right now that You are <u>in</u> the life-structure which God has planned for your experiential growth process. And yes you willingly entered into it, knowing it fully beforehand. <u>*You*</u> saw it as beneficial too. As we are One with Divine Mind we knew the story and its benefits. Because Free-will is PART of the Divine ONE from the beginning, we all, as perfect individualizations of God are absolutely agreeable to having the experiences *that we're having here* in this *Earth-life experience.*

It's probably *Improbable to You* that you'd **Choose** having all the Pains you have in this Earth-life. But once you realize that as a mature Center of Divine Mind you agreed to it (*to experience the depth of human life – beneficially comprehending it*) and this is the reason why You chose to live here in this three dimensional life.

When we see the cosmos as Einstein saw it, as a *bubble of Time-Space – Matter-Energy,* we may see into its structure; how God has formulated a three dimensional story within an etheric plasma called 'Universe'. See, scientists are finally admitting (*and not so clearly*) as they do not *want to sound like philosophers,* that the cosmos is **one single "object essence."** And in admitting that, they then see NO Time, and that everything is works together as a Lawful Continuum. The concept of Predestination works absolutely great within that idea. Physicists call it **Determinism**. See, they already believe in *Predestination* .. they call it **Determinism**.

Now, as a center of Divine Consciousness you naturally have the same awareness of Earth's benefits as *The One* does. So even though it seems we would not choose to experience the pains on Earth, we do realize that the deep and efficacious things being *Felt here in our Soul Expansion* are actually perfect experiences for us.

The challenges and talents that come by having your DNA, along with the family you came from and the environment you grew up in, are all held in place by a conscious symphonic divinely orchestrated reality of God's mind-forces and conscious designs. The elements of your life are designed and held in place by the Infinite Mind of our Supreme Source-Self, so at least One corner of the universe (You) is HAVING these experiences…that You are having.
Because of you the universal Divine Mind is more expanded, as You are adding To it .. adding to the sum-total of all experiences, experienced everywhere, within The All. So thank you.

Friends, it's all about *Experiencing* an infinitude of Love.. in Being … and.. *feeling, knowing, and developing* a Divine Partnership with The One .. each and Every moment.

IV. Infinite Mind Binds Everything

Living with WHAT IS And Improving It

So…what would life BE, if there were no opportunities to test our mettle, and our creativity?

Yet, when we're no longer 'ego-drawn' (captured by past pains, addictions, ineffectual habit-patterns and emotional weaknesses) it is such a freeing and empowering existence, that when we co-create our new Life-Awareness, with God's Leading, the richness that life offers, with its challenges .. are a welcome exercise for our creativity, and our problem-solving.

Ascending the mountain of life in each life is where true Satisfaction and accomplishment spring from. It's the richness of a Divine Human. For, we are Here building the Domicile of Heaven on earth, in us. Our purpose here, in the 'universe' is to bring the Essence, the Love and Will of *The One* to Materiality. You're an on-purpose Child of The One.

So *"with a wholesome discipline, be gentle on yourself"*. 7.

Also, look upon all the souls out here on your streets and byways – gaze into their eyes, savor their smiles, their shy glance downward, the giving up of their seat, the striving they do just to get through the day, and be Amazed, be Glad, and be Love in your interaction; they deserve divine credit .. and ardent kindness.

59

There is no size to Consciousness. It is infinite — there are no borders, boundaries or edges. God does not really need to be omnipresent, because 'everywhere' is in God's mind.

IV. Infinite Mind Binds Everything

~ THE TOTAL REALITY WITHIN CONSCIOUSNESS ~

It's a hard thing we're about to share. It's difficult to grasp; perhaps the most challenging communication anyone has ever tried to write. People rarely try to prove the 'All-inclusiveness' of Consciousness. So this centers on our consciousness – *which is indivisible.* See what I mean? Indivisible? .. what does that mean? Well it actually all begins with Divine Consciousness... which is yours, mine, ours and All Consciousness Anywhere, in all living things, and yes .. even in plants.

When talking on these matters – say, at a party – ask some others: Why does everything Alive have Consciousness and Breath? even plants? It may stop the conversation. The answer? God is consciousness and God is the Breath and the breathing of the entire ether-etheric invisible. There's only one of us here and that One Mind-Being happens to be Infinite, invisible, formless and eternal. Also .. a nuance of detail is – when we want to "smell, or sniff a fragrance" we breathe in, Yes? And we also need breath to taste our food, Yes? Another conundrum for Darwinians: If everything evolved separately, **why do we All SLEEP? and Dream .. even animals.** Sameness, through all kingdoms is illogical.

See *separate evolutionary lineages* means we should NOT share *Sameness* with common traits or aspects .. in any or all species. In Darwin's world we should see grotesque, mis-shappen creatures here and there. If everything comes through accidental mutations, as Darwin suggests, why do virtually all species have eyes, ears, lips, nose, brain, eye-lids, feet, tail bones, claws, teeth, stomach, sphincter muscles, sperm, ova, uterus's and placenta, with mother's milk? **Why is there a Sameness** in all these accidental creatures – *if from a random and different lineage?* We don't even KNOW that there should NOT be this sameness. **Similarities** is one of the greatest proofs *Against* 'random evolution'.

God does not really need to be omnipresent, because 'everywhere' is IN GOD'S mind. The universe is in Divine Consciousness. *God is Not **In** the universe*, otherwise the universe would be larger than God, and actually, as Yoda says, '*Size matters not*'. It's all in Divine mind.

There is no size to Consciousness. It is infinite – there are no borders, boundaries or edges. Many wonder what's at the edge of the known universe? It's Divine Consciousness of course ... unexpressed!
We are getting closer to 'indivisible' yes? (Unable to be divided).

I will not attempt to prove Divine existence here – it's all throughout, and comprehensively explained in my book *Breath of Light*. Suffice it to say, all things are ideated-emanated from Divine Mind-consciousness (The Source) which is fully infinite. The brilliant aspects, parameters, colors, permutations, textures, substances, temperatures, feelings, images and beings are all from, and within Divine Imagination. How do we think everything turns out so perfectly in balance for existence to even BE, let alone be so wonderfully and lawfully maintained, and, so beautifully In Place. *Life is a miracle in its "principled poetry" everywhere.*

No one in atheistic circles has or *can explain* consciousness (*especially not in plants)*; Darwin wouldn't touch it. In fact Darwin began his book 'The Origin Of The Species' with an already living cell. Why didn't he explain how life started? He began it with an already existing universe, galaxy, solar system, and earth in a very perfect form. Why did he not explain the origin of ANYTHING? In reading his book, you will not believe its simplistic nature. In one chapter he discusses shoulder blades, another ankle bones; another 'proclivities'; so he merely postulates (from way too few examples) the most elementary assertions (*yet he does not Have or offer any Proof*). If you read his book you'll be *embarrassed* at the lack of mental acuity in 'evolutionary ideas'. One begins to realize that students over 160 years have just 'swallowed' an *unthought-out* idea.

And no one's ever explained why every thing **breathes.** No one ever postulates why electricity *Runs every Living thing* in ever present nerve-neuron-fibers. Why does electricity run everyone? Once we grasp quantum physics we see that every particle of time-space matter-energy 'Pulses with a minute frequency-vibration' every nanosecond .. in all particles of existence (as a living heart beat in God's Mind); and we soon realize that every thing Does breathe, in its own way. Ask anyone: Where does this 'Infinite' tiny Vibrational Pulse throughout the cosmos, *Come From?* There will be No answer coming. Consciousness *like God* is Omnipresent. God IS Consciousness and Consciousness IS God. They're the same thing, only maybe no one ever *said that* to us before.

IV. Infinite Mind Binds Everything

Had we just used Consciousness and God as synonyms all these centuries it would be a lot easier to put forth this challenging communiqué, that's soon to be shared here. We have to postulate *backward, backward ever backward* to before any definable existence had existence. Go back in your creative imagination to when only Divine Being as Consciousness was alone, planning, in a vast empty Unexpressing awareness, and see that all God had to manifest with, **was Consciousness** [Self]. Before every thing Was nothing but Divine creative planning was going on. Now we may make the leap. Given, you got the idea that precedes this sentence, you may now say you understand how everything is IN consciousness. It's all miraculously held in Divine consciousness now (see chapter one). Like you know the rules of a game you're playing while you play it, God holds everything together in His Lawful mind, for our benefit, our use, our learning and pleasure (*and His-Her's too*) as He-She permeates *all* identities, personas, life forms, images, feelings .. Realities.

What are we driving at? Even those things that are called hard objects like a rock, billy club, castle or mountain are held In Mind, By mind, for Mind, As Mind, with Mind, and are of God's Mind. Air, rain and clouds are as well. So are natural laws in the cosmos held there too– gravity, light-speed, the inexplicably *exact* atomic force-ratio, is *present omnipresently* – in every atom in the cosmos. See the *Weak Nuclear Force is 10 to the -10 times weaker than the Strong force in every atom anywhere.* Your car, shoes, home, clothes, food, and dinner ware, are all projected by and held in supreme *mathematic consciousness*. Consciousness Births the universe in its formulaic entirety. There's no outside to divine mind. All is held In consciousness, even You. Here's where we get down to it.

Time does not exist. Science knows this. Time cannot be found in the cosmos, in physics, astrophysics, not even in mathematic equations. Time is OUR 'feeling' of Sequence in consciousness. 'Sequence' is merely God's story unfolding forward. All that IS the universe or ever was, is a Continuum of matter-energy in a holographic *Conscious Etheric-Plasma* of divine structure – expressing as *vapor, fire, liquids, solids, energy, Space, and You* (and it's doing this sequentially).
'Space' is an Essence too, to hold other things.
Scientists can see structure ***in It*** as well.

If we don't see that intelligence permeates everything including all particles in the universe, we are not seeing that a Divine wisdom guides everthing. Scientists know that all cosmic elements, such as hydrogen, carbon, oxygen, gold, etc. are made up of whirling energetic vortices – protons, electrons, neutron, muons, quarks – however No one has ever explained [nor will they ever explain this miracle] why they come together constantly to create the 92 cosmic elements. Why 92? Why Adhere?? For instance, when Carbon-60 has a defined structure of 60 atomic structures of the carbon atom, all adhering together – making one of the hardest and strongest materials in the universe; why does it stop adhering at 60? Why does it say No More? Why not 61.4? Who tells it to stop collecting atoms at 60? Why is it formed in the shape of a fullerine or geodesic sphere? An actual sphere? YES! Wow. It's done this for 14 billion years.

This is the same wisdom that congeals all particle-substances in the cosmos. They come together to form the variety of all substances in the universe. NO One asks "WHY" do they Know to come together ...and then adhere together for a duration of time, to BE Available for all cosmic interactions. Why does adding an extra electron or an ion suddenly make a chemical reaction occur between atoms? Who tells newly added "whirling vortices " to be *foaming, fiery or reactive,* to some other Vortice of energy? What informs these reaction between vortices? Who tells it to reveal a chemical reaction in relation to something else?

When we explain it by merely saying '*That's just the way things are*' who'd be satisfied with such a shallow explanation?
Why's it easier to say such drivel as "*that's just how things are,*" when we could begin admiring divine intelligence, that is sponsoring such esoteric and amazing realities designing chemical bonds, polar covalent constructs, making something as magical as Liquid possible? Is it beneath us to Love an Infinite One? An invisible One?
Or to thank such a One for providing everything?

The One just desired company, adventure, experience, and Love. This is why *we all enjoy* these things, because The One is giving them for this purpose. Is God's Invisibility the problem for us *giving her love*?

IV. Infinite Mind Binds Everything

Ask a secularist: Why should *Everything* be the result of dumb-luck? Why can we not ascribe an *awesome intelligence* thereto, in expressing magnificent interactive relationships in every cubic centimeter of space?

When we realize that these same intelligent and intentioned particles of Light in the cosmos, also make up our DNA [**d**esigned **n**ot **a**ccidental – *just kidding*] we then know that these same whirling vortices of light in our DNA have the informative power to grant Art talent to us, Music ability, Mathematical insight, Passion, hunger, perseverance, sexual longing, charisma, athleticism, and the nest and dam-building ability in beavers or birds, we may then see how a Divine Intention is behind the forming of all these particles, and their adhering structure, and with a transmission of awareness in each person or being [coming from the light particles we're made of] which are neatly spun and woven by God's infinite Mind, and its planned inventions, in how our bodies should work or be so complex.

Now, our choices made regarding our feelings about life are held in our Mind as well, right? Your opinions of life (till you tire of them, get bored with them, drop them or forget them) are all in mind. Your judgments are in mind...where you can ferret them out, if they're not serving you. Your anger is held in there too waiting for you to release that. Even the tree outside is IN your consciousness, and your next feeling, is in there also. Get this...
Consciousness is an Infinite Continuum, nowhere absent.
There is not a divine consciousness over there, and your consciousness over here. There is no separation. They are the same mind.

So my friends it is your consciousness that is holding the world together ... and cosmos too. I know "it is not your ego persona" that is doing this 'holding' of the cosmos (*nor even your own life story*) it's the infinite Divine One's Consciousness which has as much total intelligence and control Of and At Quantum Point, as at the galaxy level down to the tiniest, or to the biggest, God is expressing everything perfectly.
Thank God that even the most miniscule quantum particle-point of time-space is just as *guided-infused in intention* as vast portions of the entire universe are. God initiates and controls every particle for each is emanated from Divine Will. So from now on, when you Judge your

universe (*let's end that now, why don't we .. it was God's first advice to us*);
realize that you are simply judging (condemning?) an image in consciousness, an Image – *an image?* Yes and it's in a vast conscious cosmic emptiness. Everything is actually images .. in Consciousness ..
in God's Mind.

I know it's hard to grasp – even yet – but when every thing finds its "Origination in Mind" (it is all images .. In and Of Mind)
Dreams are also these images in and of mind too, right?

Your daily states and friends, pets, possessions, arguments, freeway drives, inhaled exhaust are All in consciousness too, which You get to label, complain-over, name, describe, rationalize or condemn.
It's all your assessments, that you fight with, and /or have to deal with each day (each moment).

My friends, cease judging, relax back into the quiet of observation and witnessing and watch things come together or 'fall apart' as the case may be. See, the truth is '*You are pure Consciousness*' and that consciousness samples an entirety of infinite awareness, yet it's operating *as You right here* in your life.
It's Divine Consciousness. The problem that we have, is identifying as our body persona. We believe we're Susanna, Ken, Tomas, Maria, Wu Lei, Sven or Mubatu. That's a temporary garment you're wearing.

Yes, it lives and breathes (*but the living and breathing are what You are actually doing*) and the "Life being had, is just the 'ME' persona" we get to *feel and experience*, *identify* with, *learn* from and *have compassion with*.

All of this is IN God's Consciousness, which is Your consciousness.
So even though your neighbor, the dog, or garbage truck may irritate, it just shows you — you're a very proficient center of consciousness.
You are formless infinite, unconditioned Divine Awareness.
You have *Everything* ... within Your consciousness.

"Welcome Home. Nice place ya got here."

IV. Infinite Mind Binds Everything

Cease judging ... relax back into the quiet
of observation and witnessing,
and *watch* things come together...

~ *Practicing the Presence of God* ~
This has been practiced for many ages,
by the Masters. It is practiced and adhered to
daily, in every thought, word and deed.

IV - A Path Upward

*L*ook now at the Unification Process between the Inner One
and Outer one, to bring your Heaven into your earth.
The One is an infinite intelligent Omnipresent Loving Being,
and is therefore inside YOU.
The One, living inside you, can therefore be felt, and so,
desires communion and experiential oneness with You.
This is accomplished Consciously by you… and that is the key,
to practice this Purposefully… Consciously…
through several experiential means.

We call this: *'Practicing the Presence' of God.*
This has been practiced for many ages, by the Masters.
It is practiced and adhered to daily, in every thought, word and deed,
in which we participate.

Look anew, at the word and the concept of Meditation.
Meditation is listening for, and communing silently with,
your Divine One within. This creates Stillness in mind and body.
It extends your awareness into a quiet, hyper-receptive state.
Now, breath-work before and during meditation is a very powerful
entré to sublime states of meditation.
So… Meditation shuts out the world… and sounds…
and others, although one will find, with practice,
that one can enter a beautiful state of meditation
even at a bustling noisy site, in the middle of a city.

However, the purpose of meditation is to be single in the intention of
Oneness with our Divine Inner, in quietude…Listening, and NOT to
ego-mentation, but perhaps, just to our Breath … to its hiss and hah…
and the glorious Silence, in the deep of your Consciousness.
Listen to the still small voice.
If ego-thought arises, go back to focusing on the Breath.
Practice this opportunity of Divine Oneness morning and evening
in significant silence, just you and The One.
Next, consider anew that which is called Prayer.

That Which is Called Prayer

Prayer can be practiced without ceasing.
It is a 'Proactive' communing with your Divine inner.
It is done by making communication to the Divine One within, during the day; laughing together at an amusing sight; sharing a beautiful sunset together; or consciously sharing the taste of delightful food. It is smiling into the eyes of another… looking into the eyes of The One in that person too.
In summary, it is the simple sharing of any and All experiences consciously… with your Divine One within… as you live each experience.   Share. He-She is listening, and loves to share.

This is why it was said of Enoch:
'*Enoch walked and talked with God, each day of his life, for 365 years.*'
This 'co-operation' is…an actively pleasurable sense of camaraderie with the Divine One in YOU.
Prayer is not just saying, "Please, I want."
Prayer is also saying 'I love You.'
It can be and Is a constant communing with our divine intelligent loving Life force who directs and operates our body temple, on our behalf. Realize.

You do not TELL your body to do all its endless services daily.
It is Divinity which operates ALL the activities of your body's hundred trillion cells every millisecond, without your taking-thought over any of it. When one knows that each of our 100 trillion cells performs multitudinous functions <u>each</u> second, then one realizes that some 30,000 trillion cellular functions occur every moment of the day throughout our body, and WE are not directing any of it.
In fact, we are mostly unaware of it all.

What intelligence IS guiding the all of You? *The One* of course.
Trillions of functions per second requires vast intelligence, communications, systems coordination, back-up systems, and Infinite synthesis of data. Truly we are in-tow in these bodies.

All WE have to do is ***manage our personality,*** while the Divine One

V. A Path Upward

inside us takes care of <u>all</u> other matters of existence on a micro-second to micro-second basis. Our work consists of managing the Persona, which we call 'Self' and, keeping the 'Ego' where it belongs –
in the 'Past' simple awareness of our life.
We really have very little to do regarding the physical activities
of these marvelous and miraculous temples that we live in,
except to eat the food which we so enjoy.
The body heals itself with consummate wisdom, inexplicable to us. Yes?

Our talents, the skills we develop, and the abilities born into us
in our DNA, are gifts the Divine One within, has given to US —
to the Self-hood out here in the universe.

So let your moment-to-moment communication start and conclude
with the Divine One inside of your awareness, morning and evening.
As you walk through the day <u>Do</u> this 'Praying without Ceasing'.

It will lift up every moment, and every activity of your day to do so.
Imagine being excellent in all things. And ask any questions to your
inner Partner that you may have on an ongoing basis,
whenever they arise, and listen for, and wait upon the answer.
When the answer is received, do it peacefully without worry.

When PRAYING

*I*n prayer, <u>If</u> we pray out loud to be seen of men, in a public show,
we may be judged by others as *self-righteous* and our public words
cannot be honored by our inner Being anyway.
For public words only "serve our ego" which exacts its own price,
feeling false rewards. Many words do not make a prayer.
But just this — 'I AM' can move mountains of trouble.
Prayer is not made with the lips, but with the utterings of the heart
— in its yearning for Oneness.

True prayer is accomplished in Interior Privacy–in the secret place
of our Soul and Spirit.
When we're in *communion* with our SOUL, our elevated Consciousness

— and when we are One-with our SPIRIT —
the Universal, Cosmic Breath – we then rise above the ego-state...
as we enter a Divine Silence to Create.

In our Divine Center we REST from our personality and we are in touch with Peace. In prayer we calm down. RELEASE your worries (they prevent your entrance into your Soul State).
REST peacefully in prayer – in confident expectancy – knowing it is a Divine pleasure to give you the whole Consciousness.
True Prayer creates a delightful Integration between our personality and our Spirit-Breath. In truth, the Answer to prayer exists before the prayer is made, and it is yours, before you claim it. Your Desire is its herald – your Vision its promise. Effective Prayer concludes with CONFIDENCE – (with resolution that is Felt).

In powerful prayer we "see or feel the outcome" of the prayer inside our Being and this creates a Joyfulness, and then we FEEL 'that it's already done.'
We realize the Divine Presence has gone ahead of us – before our vision — to accomplish the Purpose.
It is when we feel that click of joyfulness.
But do not UN-do it all later on, with anxiety worrying over it.
Your Joy is the sign and your Peacefulness regarding it, marks its certainty. When Divine Being feels inner Peace and Gratitude IN us God's power is released. This is because our Inner Unification with IT occurs inside us. You see our Soul (*Divine Will*) Unites with our Spirit *(Cosmic etheric Creativity*) then ever radiating Power and ever-Flowing Divine SUBSTANCE move Into our inner Vision (*the joyfully nurtured "interior event"*) and its manifestation is then brought Out. Create by becoming One-With...your Desire. It is a realization and a feeling.

Prayer is not about 'asking for' or saying 'I want' because the result of prayer can only BE that, 'your wanting.'
Wanting is a state of lack but *Gratitude* is an experience of being whole.
We shall have whatever we really believe.
Everything is actually one with us already.
See it, feel it, claim it, Smile. It is All Here Now in the invisible.
WE make it visible by attracting it to us within.

We must create consciously if we wish to escape our past.
This is *'Envisioning'* in our inner mind's eye.
And it's joyful feeling seals it for us.
Prayer is about The Present, not the future...
not maybe ... but creativity Now.
It is Divine Joy to Co-Create with a `Conscious You'—
(unconscious creation can be painful to us).

YOU are a door from Heaven into this world of matter —
into this world of experiencing. You *are the outlet* for creation.
Desires arrive by coming through you.
And Know this. Prayer is unlimited.
It is conversational and effortless. Offer it up All the time.
It is for quietly expressing gratitude in every moment of the day,
regarding anything and everything. It is *continual sharin*g with God.

For it is in every moment that your Divine "Father/Mother"
(your Soul and Breathing — your Consciousness and Breath)
provide your Life awareness.. and your Breathing, in Living Life …
as your CONSCIOUSNESS and CREATIVITY
and as literally All things in your life, in gracefulness.
And just remember: Say `Thank You' at every turn.

Our Divine BREATH
One-With *The One*

*N*ext consider Anew a mostly unknown transformative practice:
 — Breath-work / 'Holy Spirit' Teachings from Christ.
These are truly, some of the most advanced and evolving 'experiential'
technologies for Divine Oneness that we can enjoy.

Understand. God's Spirit is our breath cascading in and out
of our bodies on a moment-to-moment basis.
Also realize, our bodies and skin breathe too…not just our lungs.
But when we breathe consciously…for extended periods,
we are embracing the Divine One, and in effect, we are saying
"I love you". And by <u>breathing-In</u> in Specific-Ways you create a

cleansing within your body's structure. It's taught herein *just what to do*.
Our chapter *Sacred Power* illuminates this.
This knowledge that each of your 'breath exhales' releases bodily impurities is already a well-known fact in health care circles.

However, *purposeful extended **inbreathing*** heats up the Fire in each cell of our 'body-electric'. This 'fiery' flaming in each of our cells purifies our physical bodies of myriad poisons found in our *cultures and societies*. Pollutants such as smoke, heavy metals, pesticides, chemicals, poisonous substances cannot stand in the face of the Spirit-Breath of our Divine One within, who is flaming our bodies to new and beautiful heated states of purity.

Our most etheric aspect – the Breath – *(the seeming most insubstantial)* is more powerful than matter, even our past decisions.
Do not concern yourself *with past choices* just make the sound one now.
This secret of the Breath has been a secret, kept from the masses of mankind, for eons. The 'Few' knew that the practice of the breath (the conscious breathing of the Holy ***Pneuma / Spirit / Ruach / Breath***) was a most proactive way to health and healing as well as *transformation* and *true enlightenment*. The words in italics above are different culture's words for 'breath and breathing'-- Greek, Latin, Hebrew, and English.

For just as the breath purifies the body with crystal-like rarefied cleanliness in each cell and sinew, it also purifies the ego-mind of the habit-patterns that ride heavily over us in daily life.
These propensities toward fleshly down-pulling poisonous activities will NOT stand, at the 'brightness of our returning Christ Self ' …
"*who will 'rush' into our Temple with the Breath of his Mouth*". 8.

These old patterns and debilitating weaknesses which burden us daily will be burned up and melted away from our daily life and our *consciousness*. This is the freedom and empowerment of the **Holy Breath** ("*haggion pneuma*" in Greek) (in Latin, 'breath' is – ***Spirit***) and it has been Promised to seekers for ages. Does it not make sense that your heavenly Father-Mother would create a simple path, an easy way for cleansing yourself of the effects of the world system?
And have it BE right in your own being?

Your "Holy Spirit" exercises are therefore, Breathing consciously, purposefully, for Union with the Divine One inside you.
This is Baptism in the **Holy Breath.** And it's *more powerful than you know.*

Christ taught these Holy Breath practices to transform our being.
As John 20:22 says of Christ's teaching to his disciples:
"*Christ <u>breathed</u> with them saying, Receive the Holy 'Pneuma'.*
'Enephusasen (from enphusao in Greek) means **in-breathe** *or inhale.*
He **inbreathed with them**. *He did not breathe ON them, but with them.*
The Latin 'Spirit' was never in the original *Greek* New Testament.
In the *original* Greek *Pneuma is the last word there.* It's where the English word *pneumonia* comes from (a breathing disease). *Pneumatic Tools* also originate therefrom, as they are tools that "breathe" in their work.
'Spirit' in the Latin, means **breath or breathe** (as a noun and verb) too.
'Spirit' is where the English word *re.Spiration* comes from; *Re-spirator* –a hospital breathing device--does too; and where the word *Ex-sPire* arises (*dying with no more breath in us*). *Re-spirate* and *Respirat-ion* means to *take spirit in* again and again; it equals, To Breathe.

It is interesting that 17th century translators of the Bible used the English word *breathed* at the beginning of the above verse, and then used the Latin word for 'breath' *(spirit)* at the end of the verse, isn't it?
It makes one wonder why they would do so. But just ask.
When translating for English-speaking people, why go to *Latin* anyway? It confuses the matter to use 2 different languages to translate the same word <u>breath</u> and *In-breathe* in just One sentence. Several hundreds of years of authentic *spiritual comprehension* suffered terribly because of it.

Now then, remember also that John the Baptist said, in Matthew 3;
"***I baptize with Water only, but he that comes after me...***
shall baptize with the Holy Breath (haggion pneuma) And FIRE".

What is this 'fire' you may ask? It is slowly becoming clear now.
And simple, Yes? The dawning of awareness is exciting.
The purposeful, spiritually dedicated Breath causes a 'purifying fire' within our cells and brain .. to cleanse us. Oh my. This is a secret of the ages, and even our medical communities conform its truth.

"The day of Christ (our higher identity) shall come to us with a sound, and fervent heat, and the old works shall be burned up."
And who shall stand at the brightness of his Coming? [Not the ego].
When he rushes into his temple with the Breath of his mouth.   8.

The Holy Spirit is not some 'ritual blessing' that a priest dispenses
by praying over one, by merely sprinkling water on someone's head.
Think You that the Holy Breath is actually an invisible agency of God
(which…as part of God…would therefore be Omni-Present)…
yet somehow be lacking from us at the moment of our
formal 'submersion in this breath'?
How can some part of an omnipresent God whose being permeates us
and We in Him…Not be present or available to us?

No, this immersion in the 'spirit-breath' is performed daily
by each person in her or his own Sacred Breathing bodily.
This is performed with ceaseless dedication through our daily lives
and it is performed intently with its Purpose being that of purification
in mind and body for achieving greater conscious Oneness
with the Divine One within. It is performed for Love's sake.
It is performed for Purity, Power and Capability too.
It is not performed as a rite of passage just 'Once' long ago at a religious
baptismal ceremony … NO, it is performed every day.

It's what Christ was *attempting* to convey to us. If we knew practicing
the breath Quiets our mind bringing us to inner silence– we'd under
stand the Reason to practice it. But religion changed the Holy Breath
concept to an esoteric 'non-event' calling it an etheric ***agency-essence***
"from heaven above". Religion did not want you to know that it is *your*
Breath…*Your* portion of the infinite Divine etheric essence..
cleansing your Mind and Body!

If you knew that, imagine your personal being's Purity and Power.
Knowing it we could have *transformed* earlier, say from Childhood on
.. and all through Life. Sickness could be unheard of in the future.
So…we now have a path and a methodology for absolute health and
cleanliness in mind and body. We now have a way for a proactive
pursuit of *'cleansing the Ego persona'* and its sway over us.

Yes, the breath-secret has been withheld from the masses for ages, but look at your current *bodily sciences, in your birthing babies, your athletics, your health writings, spiritual retreats,* in the performing arts – it is there, even now – this calming aligning truth of the Breath (*yet has been with held from most people for ages*). This was the secret power that Moses implemented and purified Self with in the fiery burning "bush"-*System.* BUSH is a code word for *"system of teaching yielding fruit to those who partake there."* Many of your ancient spiritual practices, which were given only to the few — to the elite or to royalty — had this sacred knowledge of the Breath, included in their curriculum. This proactive experiential Masterpiece of spiritual Breathing, when combined with Prayer, Study, Meditation, Physical Fitness and Service for others, will transform our life and our earthly being right before our eyes.

Jesus was a *Jew* and *Jewish Rabbi*. Oddly many people don't know this. His teaching to the people of Israel for the years during his ministry were all Jewish teachings, of the Jewish faith (Essene) and these people were all the same blood. He taught the Law(s) of Israel and even said, *"I came not to destroy the Law but to fulfill it, but"* In John 4 Christ says:

"The hour is coming and now is, when true worshippers shall worship God Truly in their Breath ... for the Father is seeking such to worship him. God IS Breath. and they who worship truly, must worship in their breath."

One can almost feel the texture of Jewish history *coming to a bottle-neck* when Jesus teaches all this to the Samaritan woman at the well. '*The time is now*,' he says to her. Yes, he had brought and taught all the material to which the Jews had adhered for thousands of years, but he was also bringing something new. What else would you expect from someone as inspired as Jesus? And we will soon see, in the interpretation of the *Gospel According to Thomas,* that what he was bringing was something so transformative that it makes all the religiosity of former teachings and former eras pale by comparison.

The Uniqueness Of Jesus' Teaching

It is this teaching he's giving to her, that is the *uniqueness of his teaching*. It is what set Jesus apart from the old forms and old teachings. When

John 4:23 in the King James version says, *"worship in spirit and truth"* it's hard to understand how to implement that as a form of worship. It's so abstract. However when we understand the *spiritual code-language* and that the word *spirit* really means *breath* (in Latin) we can realize how each word in the Bible even the spellings or word order, are crucial to a proper understanding and interpretation of Christ's teaching. In Jesus' words we are informed of a new and important life transforming technology, that he intended for us **to practice.** You'll notice that Jesus is *actually teaching* that **God** (*the infinite Energy-Essence-Mind-Soul-Heart of the universe*) Is Breath. And yes, your very Breath is God. It's a noun. Try the verb. God is also one-with our **breathing** every moment. Being etheric, **God is the breath** – the sharing and *Giving of* our Life. Now, with that awareness what *empowerment* may that effect?
If we can step out of our mental box (*from the indoctrination we have received in hearing the word '***Spirit***' our entire lives*) we achieve a oneness-awareness, that we much need. God is one-with us As - In our Breath.

What's fascinating is when going to *biblical* or even *ordinary* dictionaries when looking up the meaning of **Spirit:** (*it will tell us it's from Latin and related to* **Spirare**-*to* **blow or breathe**) then it will say: **1. Breath - Breathe** (*then it will say an interesting thing*) "By *implication* or **connotation** it means many other things (*that WE ascribed to it*) **soul, mind, being, divine, god, angelic, heavenly, demonic, life force** etc. See, it was Us who gave it all these *other meanings;* when it was really just **breath**. Now a real shock, is that **Pneo** the Root of *Pneuma* simply means *Breathe Hard.*

Jesus taught this breathing practice because it allows us to more deeply experience God, as real in our lives. The breath *unifies and empowers* us within and without, in our consciousness and body, our spirit and flesh, in order to lift us up to very new heights. When one understands that specific and conscious breath work has been a long-standing transformational discipline taught in spiritual circles worldwide, for millennia, *in the Mystery Schools of higher awareness*, we can now understand it.

Likewise Jesus teaching the Holy breath in the New Testament was meant to advance us to new heights of transformational power and partnership with God. That was the esoteric teaching he gave us. Once we know that the Divine God Spirit is our breath, the Breath *of all Life,* our oneness with the Divine Life of God becomes *obvious.*

V. A Path Upward

The Holy Breath (spirit) was not given it was practiced. Our *holy breath* has become known through all these years as the 'Holy Spirit' because the King James translators purposefully used the Latin *Spirit*.
Had they just used the English word *breath,* we all would have called and known it as the 'Holy Breath' .. all this time.
Imagine 400 years of everyone, even all ministers in all pulpits every where, speaking the '*Holy Breath*'. It would have changed us. We'd have asked **What is this Breath that we are to understand?** Jesus' new Breath teaching was not an esoteric nothing, effectuated by a simple prayer from clergy praying at a baptism saying: '*And now receive the holy spirit*'.

No it was a proactive spiritual discipline he gave us, which we should implement on a daily basis. Why was it called Holy? Simple. When we *breathe* to be consciously one with our Father-Mother God it's called the holy breath, or breathing. The Holy Breath concept also was meant to bring to the Western and European minds the awareness that breath is the *Divine Breath* and that we should implement its influential healing practice in daily life, because it is physically, and spiritually transformative. The breathing practice Jesus recommended was meant to make us more powerful, by purifying us to a finer lifeforce vibration, so we are more in tune with Divine Being in our thinking. Remember everything in the universe is vibrating, ever so gently. *Everything*. It is the nature of energy, of which our bodies are made.

This is one proof against atheism and Darwinian evolution: for a ***lively Pulse of energy*** is shimmering out in every particle of time-space and matter-energy; There has to be a *source* of it, giving its rhythmic and measured "heart-beat" (to All of existence – even to space). Since they cannot say where this energetic pulse comes from, in the infinitude, they just *brush it off* mumbling as they walk out of the room. Whenever **Causation** comes up in the conversation, godless scientists are silent. They simply have no explanation for the cause of the pulse, the cosmos, its laws, its energy, or .. anything.

Increasing our personal vibration allows us to experience the higher states of being, along with greater health and intuitive insights. Many have taught this breath work over centuries and taught that it fires up a heightened vibrational frequency for our human body and mind.

It allows us to act, live, and behave more from a realm of Lightened Energy rather than the realm of lower propensities in our ego (*programmed impulses constantly influencing us downward in empty path ways*). Those denser gravitational effects of ego-centrism direct us toward the poisons we ingest, seemingly helplessly (nicotine, alcohol, sugar, caffeine, myriad chemicals).

Just know, our Ego is a recorded continuous sense of self in our basic memory (operating as our past self-image, even in our present). The bad habits and poisons we indulge daily come from impulses that are constantly projected into our mind…by our ego recording.

Imagine living from a state of grace through this practice of the Elevating Breath, in which we operate at such a level of harmony in body, mind and emotion that we are not affected by the negative aspects of life, which bothers most everyone else on the planet.
Wouldn't it be like a slice of Heaven to live at that level, where negativities don't affect us as they use to? When we daily practice the Divine Breath, we learn to respond to the world from peaceful calm and composure. (See '*Sacred Power*' for powerful breathing techniques).

Water Baptism is Submersion, and Breath Baptism is Daily

Many of us have already gone through the Essene water baptismal ritual, or seen friends or family go through it.
Afterwards, we may not notice any difference in them or in the way they behave. We also may not have felt a tingling and felt no difference in ourselves, no change in our strengths or weaknesses or our actions. What was that 90-second ritual about…we may wonder? Did it, or does it have any real impact on us in our mind or heart-life?

How many folks have we seen get baptized and known immediately that the ceremony did nothing to change their very questionable attitudes and actions in daily life? How many people for centuries have been baptized with no effect or reality to its purpose?
Perhaps with sincere people, there is some sense of newness or a lingering inspiration that lasts for a while, buoying them up with

confidence that '*all their sins were removed*'.
But what really got transformed on that baptismal day, if anything?

Jesus said that it's our *submersion in God's breath* that transforms us. John 4 gives Jesus' teaching that the Holy Breath 'form' of worship, is a proactive, constantly practiced discipline dedicated to our partnership with God every day that God wishes for us, and that it does transform. So Jesus was indeed allowing the Essene water baptismal ceremony in which he was raised as an Essene, as a symbolic form of dying and being *buried (in water)* from an old life, and being brought up again into a new life. So there's no need to stop performing this symbolic act, as it can be a milestone for oneself and others that one has just made a commitment to start afresh with life and one's spiritual intentions.

Now look at this. The words *bequeathed and engaged* are different. This Breath is *engaged,* friends, not bequeathed. Jesus added his new, very proactive holy 'spirit' Pneuma technology /breathing discipline so we may have first hand knowledge and experience of our Divine Father-Mother Spirit-Breath *(with whom we're literally One every second)* in our breath and our consciousness. How does a daily breath/breathing make us one with Divine Life? What would it mean if we found that breathing in a purposeful manner, in specific ways, could lead us into truly deep spiritual experiences, that we never felt before?

When we realize that our every breath is in fact the Divine Breath we will look at life and our heritage differently. Just so, Christ knew that people understood the water baptism ritual *(they were practicing it)*. He added the daily Breath Worship to increase one's awareness of the infinite etheric inner Divine.

Creating the New Human Being

At the Qumran Library, in *The Manual of Discipline* (one of the famous *Essene scrolls found in the 300 caves there*) it teaches that when a man entered their teaching he was baptized in the water there, but it was Not the water that cleansed the man's soul, it was the *Breath of Light &Truth*. The water was not the effective agent in creating *The New Man*.

It was the person's breathing the *Breath of Light* that imparted the multitudinous inspirations and impartations of truth in consciousness, for .. and In one's daily conscience.

A truly noble uplifted and understanding Nature arises in us from breathing of the Infinite Divine Essence, which is Etheric.
God's spirit is etheric right?
Which is why we are in fact, breathing in a more powerful concentrated form of God's Infinite Breath when we participate in this *breath practice*. A purification occurs in us from breathing the Breath of God's Infinite Presence, (which presence we breathe in and out twenty-four hours a day already).

A healthy and continual dose of Divine Substance passing in and through our being when done for a worshipful purpose, is done for greater oneness with our Father-Mother God-Breath-Essence-Being. And practicing it, raises us to a new height of insight, illumination and physical well-being.

Consider this. If we were to compare the effectiveness of the 2 minute water baptism of five, ten or fifty years ago, against doing new beneficial sacred daily breath work (submersing ourselves in the Divine Breath during meditation and prayer) which... would be more effective in transforming our body, mind and spiritual nature…a Daily breathing in of the Holy Breath (for 30 to 60 minutes) or that one-time event from years ago?

The breath-work facilitates a cleansing of our earthly body, our life and consciousness (in our brain cells).
Health experts already know well that with each exhale we release cellular toxins. A well-knitted partnership of felicity with God is felt in the Omnipresent Breath. It's everywhere, in everything.

The Sacred Breath *(Haggion Pneuma – Holy-spirit)* is for our Worshipful Oneness with God. We experience such elevated states of being, and such exultant inspirations redefining Identity, we are forever altered.

Think. *What is your current understanding or picture of Spirit right now?* What words would you put to it as *equivalents?* How would you describe it? Realize both spirit and breath are invisible formless life-giving, and from God. They are the same word in two languages.

Freedom and empowerment through practicing the spirit-breath has been promised for ages; (*only Jesus gave it*). Does it not make sense that our Heavenly Parent would create a simple path, an easy way to cleanse ourselves of the effects of the world system …and have it be there inside us and our volitional choices – in our power base too? Read again the Essene words that Christ lived by.

*"Our Communion is with the Angel of Air; who spreads the perfume of sweet smelling fields, the rose of Sharon and the spring grass, after the rain. We **worship** the **Holy Breath** who is placed Higher than all things created.*
 *For Lo, the eternal and sovereign luminous space, where rule the unnumbered stars…**Is the Air we Breathe In and the Air we Breathe Out**. And in the moment **betwixt** the breathing in and breathing out is hidden all the **Mysteries of the Infinite**. Angel of Breath **enter deep** in me, that I may know **All the Secrets** …"*   adapted from *"***The Gospel of The Essenes***"* –
by Edward Szekely

The Holy Breath exercise therefore is breathing purposefully for conscious union with the Divine inside us, meditatively for 30 to 60 minutes twice a day. (If we **Tithed** our being in this way each 24 hour period, we'd DO this 72 minutes each morning and evening).
Being united with the Breath during meditation, visualization, I AM affirmations and prayer creates a powerful alignment with *imbuing at-one-ness* with the infinite God Presence within.
The Holy Breath is incredible, transformative, and truly uplifting.

You may ask: *H*ow does this holy breathing melt or transform our ego affiliation away from us?

Well, as we practice taking In this etheric spiritual essence, its heated perfection cleanses our mind's proclivities with a stark re-identification toward our True power Nature. Now, we relate to the new, not the old.

Our experience of identifying with an inner light
[*in such profound intensity, heat and 'effervescent ego-dismantling euphoria*]

makes relating to that old ego in the tiny persona *like a dandelion frong blown away in a summer wind*. Just where did that web-wisp go to?

Once we have **had** the experience of our Divine Beingness
[*not to mention having these experiences 'Multitudinous times'*] there's very little on Earth that compares .. or can "hold a candle" to it. And nothing has more drawing-power of our attention, than that *sublime Knowledge-Feeling* of our identity being redefined in a new light of absolute grace – and rarified exultation. The experience of this, our *Truth of Being*, is so beyond words, it is incomprehensible to us (until we have entered into it) and felt its omnipotent power.

Friends, reading about all this may entertain the mind, or perhaps make us feel impressed in it .. or significant .. but let that go. This is not entertainment; it is a divine call to our Truth, and our inner nature.

Now, you may *experientially practice* this personal *Power & Purification* every day. We are to simply apply it. Then .. watch what happens In you and To you – to your self image, your inner clarity, your omni-present 'cleanliness inside,' your intuitions, your energy and Joy. Oh my.

It is our powerful Self, wishing to inhabit an *upward New View* over our *tiny estimation* of life. *We're to become one with Him-Her.* The *divine One* in us '*is of too pure eyes to see imperfection*' 9--and wants you in there too.

The quotations in 'Kabala-Zohar-Yoga'

JESUS – John 14:10	1	
Gospel of Thomas #67	2	
PAUL – Galatians 3:28	3	
KAHLIL GIBRAN	4	from "The Prophet"
John's 1:9	5	
GIBRAN	6	from "The Prophet"
Max Ehrmann	7	from "Desiderata" – a poem
Mal. 3-4, II Thess. 2:8	8	
Habakkuk 1:13	9	

V. A Path Upward

The experience of this, *our Truth of Being,*
is so beyond words,
It is incomprehensible to us
(until we have entered into it).

Jesus Christ gave us spiritual technologies
that will lead us to an entirely
different experience of our Life and living.

V. A Path Upward

The Promise of 'The Dominion of Heaven' in Your Life

*T*he Reward for attaining this **Oneness** (this Love shared) – this I-AM-I-ness – is Experiencing and living the Kingdom-icile of God as a Dominion of *Heaven* (expansion) 'on Earth' (in your life). Jesus Christ gave us spiritual technologies which we shared in the preceding pages, that will lead us to an entirely different experience of our Life and living; and gives results in a rather Soon time-frame – not entire life times, but in months and years – in your life *now*.

Please Know: this is not 'religion's promise' of a blissful after-life. Your blissful afterlife is assured. As a Divine Being on an Earth-visit [in a dramatic, salient, experiential masterpiece of living and feeling] – you will return to your Divine Soul Essence afterward.
No, this here is a Promise and a Reward for right now. Our reward in our Earth-life-spirituality is not for somewhere else but right here, where we are.

Essenes teach: "***He who builds on Earth the kingdom of Heaven shall live in both worlds***". It's somewhat like a parallel dimension.
The world looks the same, feels the same, smells the same – it IS our planet Earth, and our life, indeed, but there is something extraordinarily different about it all.

Our experience of it is transformed, with a continuing sense of now-moment newness – quiet exultation.
Day-to-day life is truly lifted to newness, <u>soaring</u> above our old life.

Our senses are sharper, more in tuned, more alive and more refined than they were before. We see INTO not just Onto. And that is bliss.
Our perceptions of self, others, and plants and animals too, have more sublime understanding – deeper realizations into their being, their needs – and we also have compassion for all they go through in life.
Now, All Colors are more *beautiful*. Occasionally an uncanny *perception* of time slowing, reveals a billi-second 'gap' of light and sound in the continuum of our awareness – revealing Reality .. as mere images.

Regarding design with angles, shapes, forms, perspective –
we ever balance on the verge of wonder. Beauty is more beautiful.
The human form is seen as a masterpiece of art and science.
Synthesis of mental concepts and understanding the inner or esoteric in our awareness…comes together effortlessly. Intuition becomes a normal occurrence. At any moment of our day Spiritual insights unfold on top of each other continuously. We just know and feel so much more of the universe than we ever came close to receiving before, as well as in our internal universe.

It is bliss to sense and feel (*that we comprehend so much of all around us*) and have such joy in the perceiving, and tender insight toward it all. Our Smiles just materialize continually.

And one thing that creates immense pleasure and comfort is seeing God and God's handiwork *everywhere*. We keep saying 'thank you' over and over. And each time it is said, it's said with a smile of renewed graceful happiness. It never gets old, this gratitude.

Our business in it and our endeavors work with some unseen hand of blessing. Abundance is more a **State of Inner Being** but wealth may be included also.   It's a dimension where deals come together.
Other people bless our work herefrom. Our connections, colleagues, contacts and facilitators seem to blend together for harmony.

There is also a feeling in our body, in our muscles, our organs and our mind–that feels like a fine essence of 'physical bliss' (*if such a thing can be understood*) but our bodily being has more Joy streaming through it, as if it were happier being Itself than ever before. Muscles feel a joyful humming vibration being used.

Organs emanate a graceful frequency vibration in their work.
The sacred breathing purifies and elevates all the systems within, making them new. The etheric essence of God is transmuting the old into a newly refined, powerful purified systems *everywhere*.
And we will only mention here, extended healing in and out, and extraordinary abilities, that seem to correct or improve things which

manifest In and Through us as we ascend levels of Divine awareness. Our physical fitness is also unquestioned – it is sought out and *manifest* through life, while our health and bodily systems live, a state of grace.

We also discover our own personal healing methodology and practice. When sensing a discomfort, pain, dis – ease, or health issue, we simply place quiet focused meditative attention on the inner discomfort, for 10 to 20 minutes at a time on different days (*if needing powerful healing*) and that issue dissolves to comfort, and invisibility.
We know that our attention on an inner pain is *directing God's Mind and attention to There*, and then where *ever* Divine Attention is pointed, healing occurs. Like night follows day, **attention heals,** and Divine Attention (our focused consciousness) naturally, and always .. rectifies.

And... the most bless'ed wonderful State, of all these, is that we are in communion with our Father-Mother Divine Life Force Intelligence and in a coherent cascading interchange of Love, right here, now.
We are continually talking and communicating to the Divine within .. and The Divine leads us to the right byways, introducing us to a perfect person in our life. Yes, parking places reveal themselves.
So many things just appear effortlessly. The Divine becomes our All-knowing Partner, in moment to moment existence. And what a graceful state of confidence *That* produces In us. And our smiles and awareness of this exquisite Divine Partnership never leave us.

This Kingdom of Heaven on earth *As you, In you,* and your *Life,* cannot be described in these simple words. The words are of little effect. When one *feels* these truths of this Divine Dominion in one's life (*creating grace everywhere in it*) one will know that words are weak. But we still attempt to try, don't we? Yet the pay-off and blessing for living this spiritual path 'in focused Oneness with The One within,' is beyond any compensation that is ever sought out or described.

Enjoy ... and luxuriate
in this *Kabala-Zohar-Yoga with your Lighted One Within.*
It's your Destiny .. and your very own Being.
You may as well get there now .. and *Consciously.*

Jesus Speaking To the Apostle John In Private

Lift up your mind to comprehend these things, that I now speak to you.
And please share all this, with your spiritually endeavoring companions who,
are from the sublime unalterable Race of Humanity.

The One is the supreme Sovereign of all, existing .. with nothing prior to IT.
It is more than a God. *The One* is the Father of all – the Invisible One that is
over all – and who is imperishable – and IS the pure Light .. that no eye can see.

You should not think of The One as a god; or like a God, with aspects of ruling,
because it has no 'Rulership - Lord-Over' associations, within Its loving Self.
The One does not exist *within* any Thing (which would be inferior to It)
since everything exists Only within .. It.

It is Eternal; It does not need anything to be added. The One is absolutely complete;
and has never lacked anything, in order for It to be, Its sublime completeness.
It has always been, absolutely Whole, in its own Infinite Pure Light.

It is Illimitable; since there is nothing to limit It.
It is unfathomable, since there is nothing that can, or will fathom It.
It is immeasurable, since there is nothing to measure It.
It is unobservable since nothing has, or can observe It .. in Its invisibility.
It is Eternal, existing eternally without boundaries or form.
It is Un-utterable since nothing can comprehend it, or Its being .. to utter.
It is un-nameable, since there is nothing above it, to give It a name.
It is the immeasurable Light – pure, holy .. *Invisibly Blazing every where.*
It is perfect .. in Its unutterable Imperishability.
And .. it is not a part of some perfection, (perfectly expressed)
or some blessedness, (sublimely manifest) nor of some divinity shining.
The One is infinitely Greater and Beyond All .. of these. Yet .. It is not measurable.

It is neither corporeal or incorporeal. Neither is It small or large;
It is not expressed so we might say it is 'this much'... or say, it is 'this type'.
No one can understand it ... define It, describe it.
It is not one of the 'things in existence'; It IS EXISTENCE It Self .. and gives it.
It is not some Thing to be described, as Greater than. It is in Itself its Allness ..
and is behind and beyond All .. as It is not a part of the realm of this expressing,
nor of any sequence, of time or its ephemeral aspects. For, all that is part of
the world (or of its expression) was produced by some other transient aspects.
Time was never Its field or constraint, since it receives nothing then .. from any one.
That is an idea of borrowing. It borrows nothing – needs nothing .. from any one
or any thing. The Perfect One is inherent Majesty – as Infinite Wholeness, In Itself.

... So what shall I relate to you about the Ineffable Beingness of The One?
The One is perfect silence. It is at Rest *infinitely As, In,* and *Being* clarified quietude.
It Conceives of all, as It is before everything .. giving us ITS conceptions.
It is the Source of all dimensions – emanating and sustaining Everything anywhere,
in Its graceful unending Service and Its splendorous Generosity.
Yet we would never know about these things – these ineffable comprehensions
were it not for the fact, that The One sends messengers .. coming From
and speaking Of .. The One Infinite Father .. in their sharings with us.

Now the Perfect *Complete One* beholds Itself, in the Shining Light
that It emanates (*as on the surface of a Spring of Water*) [Consciousness] within Its
many Life forms — living in all the realms of existence, that IT shines forth.
It loves its *belov'ed reflections* on the Surface of this "reflecting conscious Imaging"
"falling in love" with the luminous droplets (*its conscious individual portions*) in all of
Its consciousness .. surrounding the *Infinite Silent One*.
Now 'The ForeThought' of The One, became an Idea in **Movement,**
as a Feminine Creator, congealing and birthing all ideas for expression
(*also in the 'Presence' of the Infinite Father*).

She is the First Power. She preceded every essence or thing. She came forth from
the Father Mind, as the *ForeThought* relating to All and Every thing.
Her Moving Light resembles the Infinite Light of the Father, yet, as a 'Shining'.

She is the perfect Power. She is the Image of the sublime Breath of moving Light –
transcending, shining, rising, descending, expanding, contracting .. so that
She is the first Power – the constructing glory of the Womb of Creativity – and the
emerging glorious "Shining forth" .. of Divine Ideation being made manifest .. *As.*

She is praised and glorified in her children as our Pristine Breath, for She came forth
from The One as "*Movement and Rest*" every where. She is the First Thought
and the Moving Image, in Mind .. Of and In the Breath – Within and Without.
And as the universal Womb, She precedes every thing. She is the common Parent,
in all humanity, as the Holy Breath... and the androgenous One in the three names –
Father-Mother-Child. And She is also the eternal realm of motion and rest, for all
invisible and visible beings .. their resting place .. and the realm of purposeful action,
wherein all beings reside to experience all things.

She asked for the five Eternities of Being. And The One *agreed.* She asked for
Forethought, Foreknowledge, Life Eternal, Truth and Imperishability. She received them.
The One entered into Her *Moving-Resting Forethought-Being* projecting forth a Ray,
not as bright as Her, but each Child of us, was a union of The One and the Mother.

~ *Jesus Christ*

Adapted from Marvin W. Meyer's translation of -- The Secret Book of John

Essene Worship Poetry

"As long as I live it shall be a Rule engraved on my tongue,
to bring Praise — like fruit for an offering —
and my lips shall be a Sacrificial Gift.
I am making skillful Music with lyre and harp to serve God's glory,
and the flute of my lips I am raising in Praise regarding
His Rule of Righteousness.
Both Morning and Evening I am entering into this Covenant with God
and at the end of both, I am reciting His commands…
and so long as they exist… There will be my frontier,
…and there, my journey's end.

Therefore I'll bless His Divine name (I Am) *in all I'm doing and saying*
And before I move hand or foot, or whenever I am going out or coming
in, or whenever I sit down, and whenever I rise up or even lying on my
couch, I am chanting His Praise.

My lips shall Praise He Who Is *as I sit at the table which is set for all*
and before I lift my hands to partake of any nourishment,
from the delicious fruits of the earth, I'm performing this love
of Him-Her.

Even when fear or terror come, and there is only anguish and distress,
I will bless and thank 'He Who Is' for the wondrous deeds
of His creation story, and I am meditating upon Her power,
and I am leaning upon His mercies all day long. For in His hand
is Justice for all who live …and all Her works are true.

So, when either trouble comes, or salvation,
I am praising God, just the same."

Adapted from *'Praising God at All Times'*
[column 10] from *'The Manuel of Discipline'*
found at the *'Essene Library'* — in Qumran, Israel
THE DEAD SEA SCROLLS

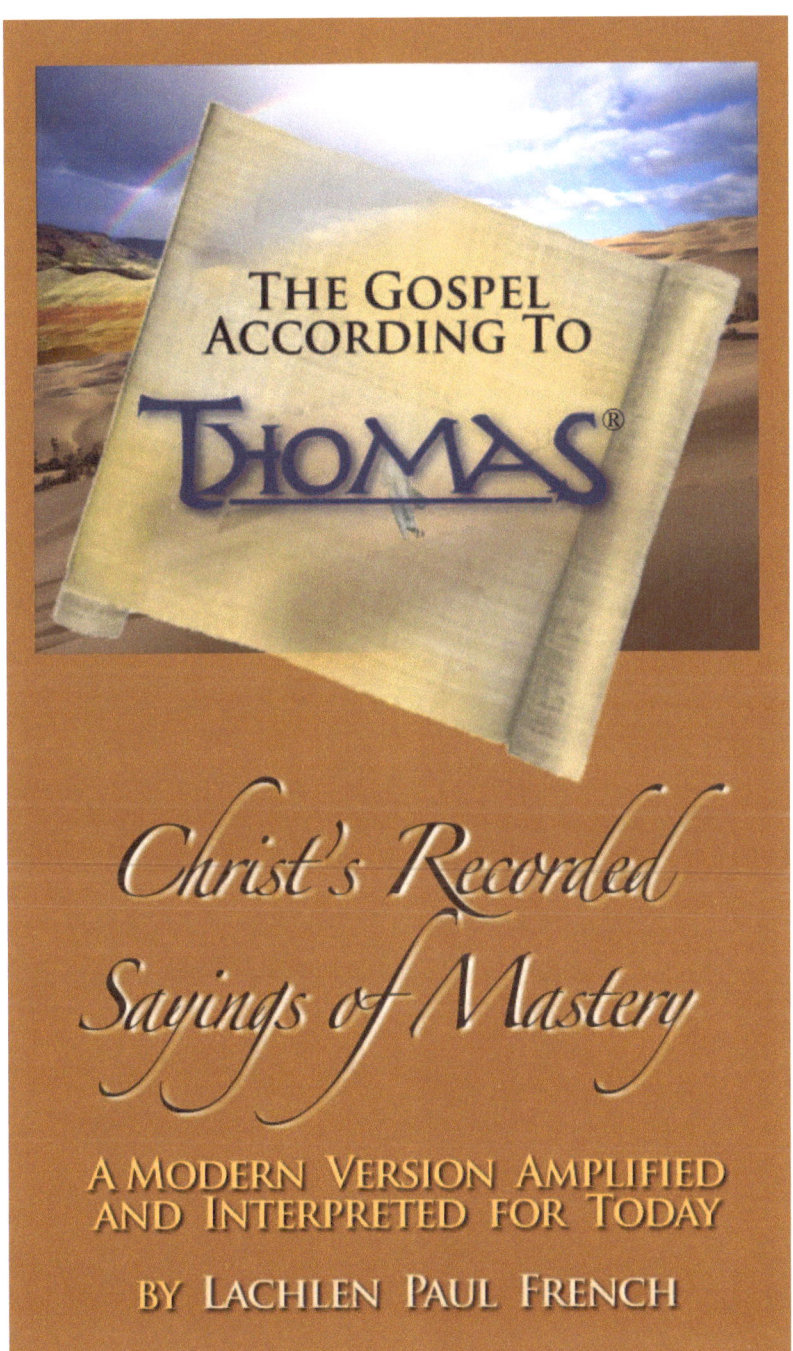

The Gospel According To Thomas

Christ's Recorded Sayings of Mastery

A Modern Version Amplified and Interpreted for Today

by Lachlen Paul French

My Father and "I" are one,
but my Father is greater than "I".

The GOSPEL ACCORDING TO THOMAS

Amplified and Interpreted for Today

TABLE OF CONTENTS

CHAPTER TITLE	PAGE
1. THE DECISION: TO JOURNEY BACK TO THE LIGHT	99
2. LEAVING THE WORLD BEHIND..	115
3. THE GROWTH OF THE INNER CHILD	123
4. THE PATH OF GRACE: FRIENDSHIP WITH THE DIVINE	129
5. THE PATH OF ASCENSION: *Uniting Spirituality with the Outer LIfe*	135
6. LIVING AMID THE CHALLENGES AND TESTS	145
7. REUNIFICATION: YOUR DISCIPLINE AND DESTINATION	151
8. THE KINGDOM OF HEAVEN: *Our Ever-Expanding Expansive Awareness*	159
9. LIVING DAILY THE LIFE OF TRANSFORMATION	169
10. THE TEMPTATION: WHOSE TEMPLE IS IT?	179
11. THE SOLITARY ONE: *In the Light*	187
Page /Verse Locator	194-195
Quotations in "Thomas"	194-195
Sacred Power For Purification and Elevation	197

The Gospel According to Thomas discovered in 1945, was shocking news. Yet 95% of us do Not know about it *still*. As the 1st biblical book found in centuries, *Aspersions* were cast upon it instantly by the church, even before studying it *(not very scholarly)*. When first reading this gospel from Christ's brother, Thomas, from carbon-dated 2nd century scrolls *(like the earliest New Testament books)* I was amazed how similar its quotes were to Christ's quotations in the Bible, yet different in subtle, mysterious beautiful ways. Many are incredibly similar, some new; some different; all fascinating. They were so similar to the Bible, some experts postulated **Thomas** may be the "Q"- *or 'Source document'* from which Matthew, Mark and Luke arose. As I began studying it I saw that the biblical Code Words I studied for years, are used in *Thomas'* 114 logia; so I realized this gospel *too* was written in the language of metaphor. This code language is revealed in Mark 4 when Jesus taught his disciples about it. He teaches there the word **Soil** is an equivalent for the *Human Heart.* Jesus taught in symbol. The human heart-center of us is the Soil of human consciousness. Also *Lamb* (*meekness*) *Lion (ego), Bird (intuition), Sky, Seeds, Rich Man, Shepherd, etc.* are just some of the code words here and in the Bible.

They're interpreted here for your benefit. The 114 verses are each brief, so I expanded them to bring clarity. I also perceived another peculiar thing providing an added mystery. I noticed many passages seemed to be randomly inserted in the text with no real order (*as if compiled quickly or thrown together hastily)*; as if someone made a hasty uninformed copy. Some of the verses appear to be in a proper order, while too many others are unrelated in subject matter to the surrounding text. Still others, answer a question posed pages earlier.

One can just imagine how ordinary real-world concerns or troublesome matters might have influenced either the transcribing or collation of the thoughts in the scrolls. It may be that what we found in Egypt is a copy of a once more complete set of scroll-works, in a different order than in this one. *I believe* it was much larger, back then. The bedouin who found it claimed several scrolls *were burned for kindling*.

So to point out a few examples one can easily see that logia 14 answers the question in the first half of logia 6 (*not the second half of 6*); and verse 13 does not ask a question that 14 answers. Another example is logia 92 (*which has important spiritual implications in it*) is not appropriately *served* or related to verse 93; nor does 93 logically follow the subject in 92. So in this *Interpretation of Thomas*, verse 6 is split in half (*the logical thing to do*) with 14 answering. The salient message in verse 27 now answers 92 because it seemed the most appropriate verse in the book to follow such a spiritually portentous statement. These are just a few examples; there are many. Anyone with an eye for *Thought-Progression* can see that the content from one verse to another is not related to or served by its neighboring verse. Most of the verses are now *re-arranged* in our interpretation to reveal their meaning providing a flowing continuity of ideas, in spiritual principles which builds structure. Verses are now next to verses related in subject and/or tone, flowing together nicely from one idea to the next. So, where 'Thomas' was done in the code-imagery of ancient words – in no real order – it is now presented with coherent ideas, in a natural continuity. Because we've translated the Code here, it now enjoys modern-word clarity. It becomes relevant to people of our day, with our comprehension. This presentation is placed in eleven chapters that lead us through the passages or phases we may face on our spiritual path. This was written for 21st century Minds – for the way We read.

Our reference point in our modern culture is so unique and different in context, content, ideation, analogy and depth of scientific and historic perspective this interpretive re-write had to be done. There are so many people (too many with no frame of reference for understanding the ancient spiritual literature of 2000 years ago) it was needed. So, with great care and love it comes out to you. I was compelled to do this over years. This is a translation for our current hearts. Enjoy its present-moment *form*, and its revealed *spiritual Context*, along with its deeply *mystical contents*. You can read the original form of *Thomas* in my book **Breath of Light.** Enjoy now Christ's truly deep and most private teachings to his disciples.

Splendorous Light Within

"I shall give you what no eye has seen, nor ear heard, nor hand touched.. nor any heart received. What I give you now are the Mysteries of Being,"

~ Chapter 1 ~

The Decision:
to Journey Back to the Light

In the beginning was The WORD-Idea   [I]
and The WORD-Idea was with God   [I AM]
and The WORD-Idea was God.   [I AM the I AM]
                                                          [in all things]
All things *were made* by The WORD-Idea [I AM *That* I AM]
and outside of this WORD-Idea *Expression* was not anything made.

In Him [*in the expression of the Divine Word-Idea*] is Life,
and this life is the Light in all of humankind.

This is the true light of Divine Being,
which lights every soul that comes into the world.

Adapted from John 1:1, 3-4, 9

    "These are secret teachings of the Living Jesus …"
    ~ Recorded by Didymus Judas Thomas ~

(A note on the typesetting in this modern interpretations: All caps and /or Bold can indicate that a word may be one which is a Code Word — one of the Secret symbolic words that need amplification and interpretation. Such words typically will have an explanation immediately following them, in parentheses, to illustrate their inner significance. You'll also notice that the Interpretation of Thomas uses the line-length and spacing of poetry. This visible treatment of the dialogue between the Master and his disciples simply provides a visual setting that lends itself to an ease of assimilation. Enjoy.)

Jesus began speaking to his disciples,
and looking into their eyes, he spoke powerfully to them:
If you discern the significance behind my words,
you will not make transition from life through 'Death'
[through a state of transitional non-awareness]. 1.

If you are truly a spiritual seeker, you must seek within your deep Self—
inside your Consciousness and Breath—your True Identity;
Touching these realms you may find your original I AM Awareness
deep within you; for these are your connection Point to Divine Being ...
and they are *in you*. Finding Your center, your life will soar gracefully.
So do not cease from your spiritual seeking until you find your
I AM Center; for you will be tempted to give up your spiritual pursuit
before you find it, and you will be troubled before you find your bliss.
But do not fear over difficulties.
It is simple, if you seek enthusiastically like a child.
And when you arrive in your Deep Self,
you will be awed and in wonder,
— seeing your oneness with The All — and after being in wonder
you will reign over The All [over universal manifestation]. 2.

If like some, you pursue earthly knowledge, to know "The All"
[the Universe] but yet, if you do not yet know the depths of your own Self,
you have missed everything. For the Self and The All are One ... but the
Self is here within us, and it is to be deeply felt, and it is where *Bliss* is
realized. The Self and The All are the "within and without" of each other.
But the *Invisible Divine Self* in us, is greater; it *expresses* that which is visible.
The deep Self is our home.
It is our Origin, and our Destination, in spiritual pursuits. 67.

I shall give you what no eye has seen, nor ear heard,
nor hand touched, nor any heart received.
What I give you now are the Mysteries of Being,
for which true seekers hunger and thirst. 17.

CHAPTER 1 ~ *The Decision*

Jesus began speaking to his disciples,
and looking into their eyes,
he spoke powerfully to them...

I will lead my brothers and sisters into their Blissful Being,
one from a thousand, and two from ten thousand—yet each
shall arrive at bliss in his own time;
and no matter where they each are, they shall all eventually stand united
within this wondrous and expansive Consciousness. 23.

These secrets are revealed to those who treasure them.
Do not treat them lightly.
Do not boast spiritually, talking endlessly to others about your spiritual life.
Keep your inner spirituality as a treasure unto yourself.
Place the "coal of fire" upon your lips.
Do not let your LEFT HAND [your outer life] know.. what your
RIGHT HAND [your inner spiritual activity] is doing.
Do not spend your enthusiasm for your spiritual path in idle talk.
Do not use up your dedication for this New Mind in ego chatter.

For he who controls his tongue "can take a CITY"
[can enter a new state of consciousness]. 62.

One who is seeking within shall find Me,
and doors will be opened to one who knocks looking for Me. 94.

If you seek for your Origin within your own consciousness,
you shall discover that the Infinite I AM is truly your own Presence.
And then your moment-to-moment life purpose
can be continuously revealed to you.

This guidance will activate your transformation out of ego constraints
and it will engender spiritual creativity.
This creativity, when operating in concert with Divine Initiative,
will create True Self expression, and the unfoldment of your divine destiny.
I was asked something recently, and I did not answer you then, but I want
to tell you now the *secret of transformation* that you asked about earlier. 92.

Unless you ABSTAIN from the world and its ego-driven pursuits,
you will not find the quiet, yet expansive awareness in your Center.
Unless you honor and live the Sabbath Rest in everyday life—
resting from fearful worry, worldly lusts and the pursuit of "things"—
you will not see your Divine Soul as your living cause;
nor will you see your Holy Breath as it is — a Nurturing Expandingness.

Both Soul and Breath, work In you As you to create True Self awareness.
Soul-*Consciousness* ... is the Divine Father Life within.
Spirit-*Breath* is the Divine Mother – a moving constructive life force
within. *Meditation* makes us one-with the Mind of Father God.
Divine Breath work makes us into *Divine beings* on Earth in true awareness.
This pure awareness will take dominion over your "appetites,"
instead of your appetites taking dominion over you.
Performing *daily* the simple sacred acts of Love with your Inner, does it.

This activity will transform the Entirety of your life experience. 27.

When Spiritual Messengers visit you, and give to you your Truth
[the truth of your inner being],
for your part give them your full attention
and give them the substance of your now-moment awareness.

After they have given you their gift, learn from them
the source of their power, which is their dedication of purpose
to unify Heaven and Earth for you and for everyone. 88.

Otherwise, why have you chosen to enter The Service of Divine Being?
Was it to see the things of Earth tremble with spiritual power?
Or to excitedly watch your earthly form quiver and transform under the
influence of spiritual experiences, *like dazedly watching some magician's act?*
Are you in it to see "signs and wonders," or are you here to help others?
Did you come onto the Path to increase your material goods and wealth
and are you wanting to acquire and wear fine clothes and jewelry?
Your kings and queens and wealthy people all wear fine clothing, yet they
do not see the truth of our divine Identity.

If you are seeking fine clothing, you will not be able to find the door to the **Kingdom** [God's true domicile within your consciousness] for it requires your sincerity and your exuberance ... and your enthusiasm.
You cannot deceive your Spiritual Self.

Seek without and you can get the things of the world from the world.
Seek within and you will find your Eternal Beingness. 78.

The ministers, bishops and priests of churchianity receive opportunities to learn the keys of understanding true spirituality in their religious studies; but they seek not the real treasure.

And like the blind leading the blind, religious institutions do not teach them the truth of within-ness, and these ministers do not ferret out the keys to use them or teach them.

So the keys are hidden from the people as well, to whom they preach. And by living and teaching about outer things these ministers hinder the people with ceremonies and rituals and things — *that entertain the mind*; They ask for money, allegiance, and penance to themselves; and in empty words lift themselves up, while they hide the Divine One within each one of us. They do not lead you to the "I AM I" of your Deep Self,
but keep you down in the realm of rituals and guilt.

These religious systems mostly glorify human egos, and they subordinate one person to another person, or to an organization; which have no authority or capacity to confer justification, forgiveness, or righteousness, upon you or anyone.

That blessing comes from within you, not from without you.
But I say: The hour is coming and now is when the true worshippers shall truly worship their divine I AM in spirituality [in privacy and creativity] —in meditation and inner inspiration—(in the Deep Conscious Breath) which is the Holy Spirit's now-moment embrace.
This experiential worship unifies you with divinity:
 the earthly with the heavenly, and the body with the holy Breath.

CHAPTER 1 ~ *The Decision*

And we shall worship our I AM in true centeredness from that Fiery place within... and from our Light Being, [mingling personality awareness with that divine etheric expression] - where Consciousness merges with breathing, and Awareness with loving.

For the heavenly I AM is seeking for us to love and worship in this way, as this form of love and worship expands the "I" back into the I AM and this love reveals the Infinite in the individual. [J]

Graceful expressions of love and power will come into the world through the Visible One and yet from the invisible Infinite One.
But most ministers do not enter this Expansive Consciousness within, remaining instead in their earthly persona,
where they can exercise their control over people.
They will not allow heavenly entrance
to those who wish to meet our Father Mother God,
for they themselves would be left behind.

Therefore, be wise as serpents and innocent as doves;
Take into your own hands
The Search for entering the Expansive Awareness of your own being.

Only you can experience your own bliss
and it is only in your own being that you experience God. 39.

Troubles shall come to false teachers. They are like a dog in a cattle barn. The dog will not eat oats, but he will not allow the oxen to eat it either; and this contentiousness shall come back against him,
[as a swift kick from somewhere]. 102.

First learn this: Our Divine Selfhood has three aspects
and it exists within each of two worlds.
Each of us is a part of two dualistic worlds:
the world of our *creative consciousness,* inside us
and the world of effect, of *physical matter,* of that which appears as out here.

These two worlds are one, but consciousness actually gives birth
to the world of effect.
It's our invisible essence, our Creative Consciousness and our Spirit breath
which creates our visible circumstances, and the world in which we live.
Unfortunately, most on earth share a limiting or a fearful self-image
in consciousness. The violence, selfishness and domineering systems of this
world, inculturate earthly minds in a negative and tentative manner.
It is these poor ideas in consciousness .. our ego-self-image, and *our
attitudes,* that manifest our personal and collective experience here
on the earth plane.

We sometimes may appear to be lost in our visible circumstances,
but we are only ignoring the Invisible Power of our personal consciousness
which is our *heavenly* Aspect ... and is our divinely creative Essence.
In our permanent heavenly state of being, in our deep Self, our Self has
three aspects and each aspect serves its own purpose in our life.
Our three-sided essence includes: our **Soul, our Breath, and our Body**
as three parts of one being. These three-in-one work as one to create each
moment of our life experience.
Learn the purpose of each, and take dominion over non-conscious creation
in your life. Non-conscious creation is our trap. For we are learning to be
conscious creators — creating from love — in Awareness.

Here is the understanding of our three aspects. Let us first look at our Soul.
Our SOUL is like a father.
Our soul is actually a part of and one-with Infinite Divine Being.
Our soul is our Source of consciousness and .. is present everywhere.

Our soul conveys to our awareness our supra-conscious **"I"**.

Our soul is the starting place of love in us, our pure desires and true initiative.
It conveys our living Will into our life, creating our focused Attention,
and it is the Source of our loving radiance, which we shine upon
our loved ones, and upon our interests and desires.

Like a captain, our Soul guides our divine destiny, even when we don't
know it; and if we listen to its guidance, our Soul leads us gracefully ..
in each moment.

Now, our BREATH-Spirit is like a mother.
Like a womb, our own spirit creates and nurtures what we hold consistently in the consciousness of our soul.
With each breath, our spirit projects our "subjective awareness" directly into our lives; By manifesting that personal vision of life that we continuously hold in our subconscious or conscious mind.

Our BREATH manifests our inner "**I AM**".

Our BREATH-spirit is the secret *Intelligence* united *with-In* our consciousness creating our subconscious vision and plans in magical detail. How, we know not, but it does.
Through the activity of our spirit, we visibly see what we really feel about our self and our life.

In each breath, our spirit gathers Cosmic Substance to form our deeply held beliefs, manifesting them here. Also, our spirit produces these strongest visions and desires, whether they are positive or negative.

Our spirit is an infinite Secret Force working invisibly everywhere to out-picture our innermost world, and our self-image. This is why we need to actually groom our subconscious self-image, in inner time and creativity. So, it is our Spirit that faithfully and mysteriously produces our most insistent motivations in consciousness. Our spirit works for us in every breath breathed — twenty four hours a day.

Now, our BODY – like a child – is an expression of our *Father-Mind-Soul* and *Mother-BREATH-spirit*. Our body is a "form" in light substance projected by our soul's desire and our spirit's creativity.

Our body is our conscious and visibly formed **"I"**.

So, our body is a visible expression in form of our innermost self conception. It is a visible "I" expressed from our invisible ideas of "I AM this and that." Like a mirror, our earthly body reflects our strongest identifications and our deeply felt self–images, which we continually hold inside of us.

But realize this: Our earthly body is really more an image
of our former beliefs, and our past self-images that are still visible now.
In our "heavenly state" our soul, spirit, and light body are the
"three-in-one" operating in the now to effect some creation momentarily.
They constantly create. It is their purpose.

That which is visible now as your life, is a picture of *past* beliefs.
To improve our life we must therefore take our focus off of appearances
— off of the current situation — which depicts our past, and go within
to create anew, instead — *from our Invisible Creative Consciousness.*
If we do not go within to create anew, our past decisions continue.

Our soul, spirit and body represent our *wholeness in unification,* in the now.

They are *consciousness, creative intelligence,* and *expressiveness* in visible form.
However, in our earthly awareness these are not always consciously unified.
And this is because our ego's reactive mentation is constantly evaluating
and judging everything.
Our ego's 'attention' is focused on 'judging, animosity and attraction,'
— 'pushing and pulling' everything in our life; so that we become weary
in our agendas and we are distracted from our real creative purpose, by
habitual, judgmental likes and dislikes in the ego, (that simply drain us).

Thus, we can be asleep to our soul's voice due to this distracting and noisy
agenda in our mind, and we grow only unconsciously and slowly, and,
all too often, we manifest anxiety in our experience.

Unconscious creation is what causes us pain. It is what we are leaving behind us.
But when our attention is placed inwardly on our soul, and on our Breath,
then our three Aspects can unify, even while we are on the Earth plane; and
we grow, and we can finally Create in Love, consciously.
Our *innermost* divine Individuality called our *Christ Self,* is a Word of God.
This term *Word of God* is used in scripture to refer to our individual
GodSelf. In essence, the Divine says, "I Am This I Am" or this One,
when expressing each of us.

We are a perfect Idea of individuality within Divine Being,
and we fit perfectly into The One and its Universal Expression.

Each of us has always been a part of Divine Being's conception of Itself.
This is why we are each an Eternal Being, and why our *essence is universal*
—because of this same Oneness.
This perfect Idea that we are is what we are living up to
even when we don't know it; and it is our Christ Identity,
a divine light image, to which we are each inevitably moving.

So each of us will eventually merge our awareness into this light form
of pure Individuality. We will each eventually arrive at 'becoming'
our true essence, as the 'Word of God' Self.
It is this Christ Self of our Divine Portion that unifies the work
of our soul, spirit, and body.

It is the Image of the Divine One inside of us that always leads us forward,
and will *become* our conscious Individuality in due time.
Our Christ Self inside God's mind is made of light.
It's a projected light IMAGE in Divine Mind.
We are actually permanent Beings of Living Light; and our Living Light
is what contains the energies of our soul, spirit, and body.
When working with these creative energies, we are working with Light.
Even here on earth, it is the material of Light through which we work,
though it may not appear so, due to its earthly density.
That which appears as earthly substance is simply a shadow of the material
of light, which is "stepped down" to visibility for our benefit.

Let us now discuss a more earthly perspective.
How shall we operate in *conscious creativity* and how shall we bring about
a transformation in our personal life? Let us look at our true day-to-day
powers and our real *personal tools* within.
How shall we really understand our Triune beingness?

Think of your soul, breath, and body as the ***Love, Faith, and Power***
of your daily Self (as you express all your activities moment to moment).
These three—your *love, faith, and power* create all your experiences in daily
life. It's where you point them in this instant that makes the difference.
You see, the love within you defines the "I" of your personal Selfhood,
and this Love naturally produces initiative toward that someone or
something that inspires your fondness.

Your love comes out as **desire and inclination** and you naturally focus on the object of affection.

Now, your faith is embodied and extended as this **Focused Attention** and it also produces wisdom regarding your recipient of affection. Focused Attention radiates love, and this causes **Expansion**.

Personal Power is the resultant expression of initiating Attention toward whatever interests you.

Wherever you point your loving Initiative, and wherever you apply your faithful Attention, this is where you will find your life force Manifestation. What do you constantly stare at or continually attend to in your mental experience? Is it joy, sorrow, a poor self-image, complaints, success, or nothing specific at all?

It is this to which you give "body" in your life.

You cannot help but give body to it; it is unavoidable. Remember this: When our three aspects of **intention, attention, and expression** operate within us in concert, anything can be achieved. And when we remove any one of these energies, the activity is soon to dissolve.

So our **Intentions** start in our love and inclinations. Then our continuing **Attention** creates understanding, and we **Express our ideas visibly**, no matter what they are or where we are. Your Initiating Attention is your true power, even though your Attention is invisible.

Without LOVE (without a sense of "I") there can be no Initiative expressed *toward anything;* and so nothing would be initiated.

Without FAITH (without a sense of, "I AM focusing on this") there is no Attention expressed, and nothing can be developed *without Attention Shining.*

Without POWER (without "I" expressed) nothing can be made manifest. We call our Divine Creative Process **Soul/ Spirit/ Body**, or "I Am I."

I am This and I am That, I am.

It is where we place our energetic identification that manifests our creativity. This is the Infinite Life creating expression, as you. This is the Law of your wholeness and bliss.

SO...Unify Intention to Attention and you give out Expression. This creative process operates through you and as you.

CHAPTER 1 ~ *The Decision*

This is your true being and eternal creative purpose.
Understanding and utilizing it, is also the conscious way
to manifest a transformation out of our past choices—
(*the Past* initiating our old 'attentions').

We, therefore, shall learn this: Our three energy aspects of soul/spirit/body
manifest our creative power, when operating in Unison.
When in our daily life we work in harmony with our divine purpose—
in our Christed Awareness—our intention, creativity and expression,
work powerfully as one. Then transformation is possible and our efforts
feel timeless ... and bliss is felt in so doing.

However, if you are still unconscious of your Divine Beingness
and its conscious wholeness,
and while you are still "on the journey back" to integrating
your soul, spirit, and body .. know this one thing:

No matter where you are on your spiritual path, no matter what your
occupation or endeavor, no matter the state of your
Intention, Attention or Expression, I, your Divine Christ Light
am always with you. Yet you are free; and even if you don't believe it,
what you manifest is your business.

I AM ready to assist you in re-uniting your "divided" awareness
into purposeful power. For I AM one with you in Consciousness
and I can guide you into conscious creation
as I AM one-with The Infinite Living One ~ the Universal "I AM I"
from which we all emanate.

Think, have you not heard my Voice in the silent space of your heart?
Wherever there is three-in-one As one.. in your heavenly beingness, *This*.. is
your eternal Essence.. and it is the domain of your divine I AM I.
It is .. and ever will be in wholeness.

The Divine I AM is ever the One Expression supporting you,
and it is eternally calling out to those.. who feel separate.
(Please Answer by going within).

111

It only awaits our Conscious *'purposeful re-union'* and our willing return.

However ... wherever there are people "un-united in their beingness" — with their aspects still apparently separate — I AM by their side.

And wherever there are people journeying aimlessly in life,
I AM always with them, no matter their beliefs ...
and I will be, even as they return Home   30.

Scene from *Mystic Traveler III*

MARY MAGDALEN
Since I was young I was interested in spirituality but all the priests or rabbis I knew.. seemed not.. sincere. They didn't have that loving Authority or.. power. I may've expected too much. But it made them hollow.. they seemed.. emptier... than regular people.
   (Jesus nods a little, smiles)

MARY MAGDALEN
But YOU talk about being in relationship with the infinite invisible. How did... how does someone.. Well I know God exists that's why we..and the universe exist but.. how did you Do it? Why does the Infinite One respond to YOU?

JESUS
Very good question. No one's ever asked me that before.. not even my teachers. The answer's so simple, you may marvel at its simplicity. See.. everything comes from God's mind...especially Love and communication. Why should we think God is far away? God is the closest presence in our life and our feelings. He's 'closer than breathing and nearer than hands and feet.' And...

(Read more on page 209...)

CHAPTER 1 ~ *The Decision*

What's This? ...see page 208

Splendorous Light Within

One who discovers this truth will expand
beyond this world...in the
I AM I ... the Creative Expressive Power...

~ Chapter 2 ~

Leaving the World Behind

"I .. if "I" be lifted up from the EARTH   [from the bodily ego nature]

then you will be drawn into ME [the Divine One, in your midst]."
John 12:32

I came into the world to understand your plight and help you.
So I appeared in a body of flesh;
but I found everyone drunk with forgetfulness regarding our Divine origin.
They were "hypnotized" by trying to satisfy sensual appetites.
They were not thirsty for the *inner truth,* nor knew what they were missing.
Then my soul was sorry for humanity,
because of the sensory programming of their subconscious minds.
They do not realize that as Divine Beingness sent into the world
they arrived here empty and unfettered,
and when they leave this world, they will leave it unfettered also.
Now they are drunk,
focused on poor self-images and sensory pleasure in the exterior world.
But when they renounce the wine of the senses and the external appetites,
focusing inward instead,
they will begin seeing the truth of Who and What they really are.
They will transform from this blinded state, in bliss, and will ascend
into conscious and loving creativity, even, while on the earth plane. 28.

One who has known the world and its ways has discovered it produces an identification with the body as self, and a consciousness of self as effect, instead of cause. It is an empty identification, which feels powerless, and it leads one to the "corpse" state. However, the world-system cannot restrain one who has discovered the Inner truth, *(that our earthly essence is One-with Divine life)*. One who discovers this truth will expand beyond this world in the awareness that our conscious life and form are the invisible and visible light – The I AM I the Creative Expressive Power—which cannot end up in a corpse. 56

People think I have come into the world to bring peace to the world.
They do not know I bring division, to sift the true
from the false identifications in human awareness.
I bring a spiritual FIRE [the Divine Breath] to BURN away the beliefs
that there is "distance and separation" between Divine life and Human life.
I AM giving this spiritual FIRE (*awareness of breathing divinely pure Breath*)
so that ascendance over a body-mentality may be achieved and true
identification with Divine Spirit may be enjoyed. This true identification
frees our awareness, and reveals to us our Light Essence.

Also, I bring a SWORD (earnest, incisive intuitive discernment)
to SEVER the "binding cords" of limiting 'ego beliefs' from Living Souls.
Those who receive my SWORD are bestowed with the gift of Divine Insight.
I tell you within a person's *mental household* there's confrontation going on.
That is, within us there exists our three divine aspects as a
"Father Mother Child."
These three aspects are our *Soul purpose, creative Spirit, and self Expression;*
and these three work tirelessly, attempting to transform the ego's reactive
mental habits. Opposed to this transformation, there is also within us the
hypnotic, negative belief in separation to which man's ego, holds onto.

Mankind thinks he lives and dies alone here in this world, that he is
cut off from everything *that everything is separate* from him, and somehow
opposed to him. He believes he is not one-with the Universe, but separate.
He believes he is incarcerated in the world, that he is inside the Universe,
not knowing he is an aspect of it. It is a total belief in 'separationism'.

Mankind believes in duality. He believes in his mind and his ego,
and that he is in two-ness.
He thinks his body and soul are two distinct and different things.
He does not know that his within-ness gives birth to his without-ness.
He eventually will realize however, that he must unite his within and
without and that he must unify his Heaven and his Earth
if he wants to experience Heaven. He must bring a spiritual consciousness
to his fleshly work, to each thought and act, so that his outer life may,
indeed, be one-with his Inner Guidance.
He must work out his own salvation with reverence and submission

to his Inner Self. He must see everything as different aspects of this true
Oneness. He must realize that the entire Universe is alive with intelligence
and loving support, in a divine infinite variety, and with endless living
expression. He must see the Universe as his source and his ally..
and that *he is IT in expression.*

Until this is done, the 'unenlightened son' [*the two-ness of body mentation*] is
opposed to the Father's triune Oneness: [I AM I of Soul, Spirit, Expression]
So they appear to stand apart, this ego of flesh and this light of spirit, and
as long as "the son" has eyes closed to this truth, he feels weak and alone. 16.

One man said to Jesus: "Tell my brothers to divide up my father's
possessions with me." Jesus answered: "Am I one who divides things up?"
Looking at his disciples, he asked:
"Do I divide things up, or do I unify them?" 72.

I tell you, if someone believes his father and mother is of this world,
his belief shall make him an illegitimate child
of his Original Self in Heaven [of his Divine Consciousness].
For his belief separates him from his true origin,
and his opinion separates him from his spiritual sustenance.
If one believes that one is a human creature, he is tied to that belief. 105

Sadness comes to those whose identification is with their flesh
and whose individuality is tied to their ego-personality.
They hope that good fortune will somehow come to them like magic,
through some good luck, or that a Divine Being somewhere at a distance
will randomly or periodically "smile on them." They do not know
they must awaken to their interior powers and guidance, to unite
the leadings from their divinity within to their human activities without.
They must consciously unify their Father-soul to their human desires
and their Mother-Breath to their outer behavior. They must find the
blessing that soul and spirit bring to each moment of life's activity.
Without this unification, there is quiet sadness around the soul, because it

has no harmony with its unconscious bodily expression and is therefore
unfulfilled with unconscious creation. *Consuming the wine of the senses is an
attempt at escaping this sadness.* The soul hopes its fleshly persona with its
base identifications will at least moderately *sustain itself til unification occurs.*

I tell you, un-united with its true being, this earthly persona
shall remain under the power of its painful beliefs and its fate.
It shall be subject to time and chance, and it shall pay its uttermost karma
regarding these beliefs. But those who unite their "earthly doings" to that
pure consciousness in their Center. shall rise above their past debts.
For in throwing off the darkness and selfishness of ego-programming,
they shall ascend to a new level of existence in authentic spontaneity,
feeling bliss in each breath, and finding grace in each deed.
Then with that Inner Guidance of the moment, they will actually
leave their karma behind, and they shall take dominion over current
circumstances, with Conscious Creation. 112.

One who has known the world understands the limiting identification
the world has with the body as Identity. But one who understands
the limits and error of identifying self as the body, and as effect
will rise into the Divine Initiative of their Soul, becoming powerful
in Awareness, and will transcend 'the gravity' of the ego system. 80.

Here is a parable to illustrate how we should honor our Inner Self:
A SAMARITAN [*who to Israelites, was a second-class alien, minority person*]
was CARRYING a LAMB atop his shoulders [was acting spiritual]
while WALKING the ROAD toward JUDEA
[while moving toward spiritual integration].
Jesus asked his disciples: "What are the Samaritan's intentions?"
They said: "He will slay the LAMB later, then he will eat it."
Jesus replied: "While the LAMB is alive, he will not eat it;
he can only consume it once it is dead." They said: "That's true."
[*While true spirituality is externally incarnate as Jesus, people will not
seek out their own purified consciousness but will continually seek out his;
and this is why Christ Consciousness must be individually realized.*]

Jesus said, "You too should be seeking rest on the SHOULDERS
of your I Am [in your Soul, and spiritual center]
so that you may avoid becoming corpses in this world
and becoming ripe for being eaten and then spit out by the system."
The meaning of this parable is this: *Each of us is the "Samaritan"*
and *the lamb* represents the purity of our inner spiritual Identity.
But we carry, or wear our spirituality for 'appearance's sake',
not really internalizing it, or living from it.
And as the SAMARITAN [*as the un-illumined person of this world*],
we WALK the ROAD toward JUDEA [*move toward our enlightened
state — Judea – walking the path toward that inner "I AM joy"*].

We, like the Samaritan, are in fact hoping to receive acceptance and
entrance into the HOLY LAND [into our blissful consciousness].
So as we walk, we should take into our awareness "The LAMB"
to become one-with that gentle purity beyond ego-mentation,
by rising above it and thereby cleansing our mind of old beliefs
and old motivations. *"He who dies to this world shall live in Me."*
Drop the outer one; put on the inner one.   How do we do this?

We speak less. We still our self, becoming quiet. Stillness purifies.
We ardently listen, outwardly and inwardly, and observe the silent flow
of our feelings. We practice innocent activities.
We esteem teachableness and humility, like a meek lamb.
We do this by becoming un-entangled from worldly pursuits
and by taking charge of private moments.

So we must partake of our *light within* with eyes closed to the outer world,
feeling the expressive power of our soul's purpose, and of our spirit's work.
We must then drink the "pure blood,"
[nourishing our self with interior experiences]
by sitting quietly in solitude with our Deep Self, and feeling its reality.
We must focus within on "clear emptiness" in meditative reverie,
and we must now speak the "I AM" consciously.
Then we shall *consciously and purposefully breathe the deep spiritual Breath,
for extended moments*, becoming one-with the Infinite One
whose pulse permeates creation, and whose "exhale" expands the universe.

This purposeful and conscious breathing creates a fusion of our within and without, and promotes a oneness of our breath, to our soul and our flesh.

This Breath allows our light center, the divine Self Awareness in us,
to clean us of old patterns, and to express itself.
It cleanses our cells, our heart, our body, and our brain of all impurities by releasing its loving interior FIRE. Living life in this powerful discipline becomes like swimming with a powerful current behind us.
Then our Christed soul becomes the GUIDE and the power of our external persona, creating abundance, power, and peace in our lives.

Remember the parable: *Except a seed-shell rots away from the SEED when it's fallen into the SOIL, the seed shall not bring forth FRUIT* [bring forth its transformation].
It must let go of its identification with the hard exterior and its old nature before it can expand and grow into its transformed state. Just so, if an individual remains focused on the temporary body-personality of this world, *and remains un-initiated to his divinely birthed true soul purpose;* and if he remains unaware of the power of his divine Breath and its fiery cleansing purpose, then in this life he shall simply age, shrink and wither as the un-evolved ego personality he received at birth,
not realizing he was something magical.

So the system will eat him up in his striving in the ego-darkness
and he will die like a human.
However, when he attends to the Inner Life, he will live like a child of God.

The key is the *transcendence, expansion, and transformation* from the old ego [*the outer personality's habits and identifications,
 inherited at our DNA birth and built up throughout life*].
Then his greater Self within will become his external self.

Our greater Self arrives by our consciously involving our
Divine Consciousness within us, to absorb the personality patterns of our personal self, so that they may be used for their destined divine purpose.

You see, there is a seed impulse within each of us.

It is a motivating vision or divine template in our center of being
and it provides to us the desire of our heart,
'through which fulfillment' we experience bliss.

Look for this seed purpose in your life. Find this personal destiny
by searching your interior. Follow your blissful feelings,
and find the grace of your life path. Quiet your brain. Simply behold
the interactivity of life with your impulses, and it will lead You.

Each of us is made to shine in a unique manner, while serving the whole,
yet flourishing within our authentic purpose.
To realize the bliss of our divine purpose, we need to surrender
our identification with the small ego—those temporary personality patterns
we currently call our self, which contains empty appetites and protects itself
with defensive and constricting habits that only prolong the pain;
and forestall what is an inevitable realization of our divine Origin.

This surrender takes place in your conscious Awareness
[*when you've actually made a decision, in the quiet humble stillness
of your interior consciousness of Self*]
that you will **consciously partner** with Divine Being.

You will then be en.rapport with that intelligent, loving, expansive
life force in your center of being, and It will care for you
by empowering all that you do.
All of this occurs when you care for your mind and body,
producing purity in your activities. And by Breathing On Purpose.
Create purity on Purpose, in body, mind, and action. 60.

Then Jesus summed it up saying:
Be passers by in this world...stay centered; focus on your inner self. 42.

Splendorous Light Within

So through your powers of observation, you will
discover your pure awareness within...
Then you will experience bliss
and clarity of purpose in this world.

~ CHAPTER 3 ~

THE GROWTH OF THE INNER CHILD

"Behold! I stand at the door and knock, if anyone hear my voice, and open the door, I will come unto him, and sup with him ... and he with me."
Revelations 3:20

Often you desire to hear the words I AM now expressing to you.
But days will come when you will have no one to teach you,
and searching for me shall not find me.
So through your powers of observation, you will discover your pure awareness within, where your Spiritual Presence is, and you will become one with it, and you will attain wholeness in the single One
[within your loving and infinite presence].
Then you will experience bliss and clarity of purpose in this world. 38.

You see, being human is like being a skillful FISHERMAN.
The fisherman casts the NET of his meditative focused attention, into the SEA of his infinite Consciousness within himself *[into his Source of ideas]* and he draws out of this SEA *[out of his mind]* many SMALL FISH *[his attention is cast upon unimportant subconscious thoughts, beliefs or opinions]*.

However, if the wise fisherman discovers among these many "thoughts" the LARGE FISH *[discovering I AM Awareness* in his own consciousness], he realizes that The Divine lives in and as one's very own Self; so he throws the smaller fish *[lesser religious ideas]* back into the Sea and focuses only on the fact that his being is in fact Divine Being living each moment.
Then happily and peacefully he focuses on this greatest truth and it becomes his moment-to-moment guide and his ever-present reality.

So with joy he continually contemplates this one expansive truth
as he lives each day.
If you understand about this constant contemplation, then do it.   8.

Disciples asked Jesus: "When you, who are our spiritual teacher, leave us, who shall become the leader of our group?"

Jesus responded: 'When you have left behind your old idea of self
and have unified your soul and your flesh, your morals and your activities,
and like an athlete have melded your mind and your body —
and your purposes and actions — so that you make an integrated,
harmonious presentation of yourself in word and deed,
then shall you arrive at a State of Grace, becoming justified, becoming the earthly BROTHER of your inner Soul...in the PLACE of the OLD MAN identity [the former identifications with ego].

You will then be a CHILD of LIGHT, who needs no human leader to guide you." This is the Reason why this whole system of heaven and earth came into being. 12.

His disciples asked: "*After you're gone, when will you appear again to us, and when shall we see you again?*" He answered:
"You shall see the Christ again when you see it within your own Presence. Yet a little while and the world shall see me [*the external Light*] no more [A] but YOU will see me; For the I AM and the I [Lighted Consciousness] will make our dwelling place, in You and your individual Awareness." [B]
When you finally shed shame and guilt from your awareness,
it will happen.

When you stop thinking about mental concepts of God,
pondering Divine Being itself [*becoming aware of your soul's voice*],
then you will experience this true Self.
Take all the old thoughts about spirituality, which you wore mentally,
which like old clothing draped over beauty, concealed from your awareness that graceful Living Being that you truly are.

Now then, cast away the old conceptions of God from your mind
and trample them joyfully under your FEET [*under your new understanding*] This may take time and experience in solitude...
so apply yourself to its unfoldment.

Replace old identifications by *living differently*
with a new routine of activities in each day.
Then build on these new activities, always adding new patterns to your life.

True spirituality is not about simple church going but a loving interaction
with your Divine Being within … and your neighbor without,
who also is a manifestation of God.
Develop a new schedule for each day *rather than one not benefitting you now*
This will create beneficial patterns for you to grow with.
Building new patterns allows you to leave behind old, unprofitable ones,
until you can live in now.
You will then rise above the old inculturated patterns, as you rise into the
spontaneity of now. Then, like a child in summertime, you will be free.

You will then see the *Child of the Living One inside your own Self* Awareness
and you will see your Light Being [*your Divine "I"*] as your true Identity
and *you will no longer, serve that ego-persona* and its restricting enslaving
habits. Then fear will no longer be a part of your consciousness. 37.

His disciples said: "Your brothers and mother are outside." Jesus answered:
"Those who live and act from the expansive Consciousness within
are my true family. They enter into the divine HOUSE [our inner being]
as I do and they reside where I reside." 99.

He who does not love more his heavenly I AM—his soul and spirit—
his Mind and Breath — over those who are called the earthly father and
mother cannot follow me into the expansive realm of our divine beingness
due to their worldly focus and those in it.
But he who does not love those here, who are called dad and mom, as I do,
cannot be like me and do as I do.
For they must love the Divine Life in everyone.

My earthly mother brought me into this world of death,
but my heavenly Mother [my Spirit Breath] gives me life eternal.
The two are one, but the heavenly is greater than the earthly. 101.

Simon Peter then spoke up:
"Mary Magdalene should leave our inner group, Master,
for the nature and requirements of this life are too difficult for a woman,
who is beholden to others and encumbered with many things."

Jesus reproved him: "*Women are just as worthy as men.*
I shall lead her, as I have you, and add unto her the MASCULINE aspects
of the soul—loving purposefulness, single-mindedness, and initiative—
that she may enter into expansive Awareness,
becoming one-with that initiating soul-state as you all are just entering, too.
"For any woman who balances herself with the masculine nature of the
soul, *as any man who balances himself with the FEMININE side of spirit—*
— wisdom, nurturing, and creativity—and becoming unified,
shall enter into the expansive Awareness of their unified soul/spirit/form
and They shall find.. their divine destiny.
They shall consciously exercise divine initiative, creativity, and expression
in this world; and they shall operate from
Purposeful Love, Wisdom, and Power." 114.

Whoever cultivates words from my mouth inside themselves,
whether male or female, shall become as I AM;
for there is no partiality in Divine Being
and the I AM within him or her shall become the Higher Identity *in them.*
For them, the mysteries will reveal themselves,
and they will come to know the truth in all things. 108

But they pointed to a GOLD COIN in the basket of a nearby tax collector
and said to Jesus: "***But Caesar's men endlessly tax us. How can we ?***"
He replied: "Render unto CAESAR [the world system] what belongs
to Caesar. Give it its requirement. Making war on the Roman system
causes pain and potential death.
Do not create new pain trying to change it for your own ends;
For your kingdom is not of this world system, anyway."
 Change your awareness of self, be born anew in consciousness,
re-identify with your breath not the body; and your 'kingdom'
shall transform right before your eyes.

CHAPTER 3 ~ *Growth of the Inner Child*

You cannot even comprehend the bliss created by the beauty that exists all around us, right now. And so, you shall help your brothers more in this manner, than with any ego struggle in the outer world. those are for egos to keep themselves busy .. engaged .. but you .. keep focused within.

Then, You shall become a Light to them, and you will help them rise into their own bliss. Then they shall help others, too… and it goes on and on. Each in their own time will find and live their truth.

Therefore, render unto God *[your Deep Self]* what belongs to God *[your inward focus]* and give to your Christ Identity what belongs to it, this TEMPLE persona to govern. 100.

From morning to evening and evening to morning...
Focus on your interior Presence
while living each moment...

- Chapter 4 ~

The Path of Grace:
Friendship with the Divine

"Seek first the consciousness of God, and God's purpose for you, and all things shall be added unto you." Matthew 6:33

From morning to evening and evening to morning do not THINK fretfully about your external life.
Do not THINK anxious thoughts about food, money, appointments or any of the things concerning your outside world.
Fretfulness brings you down.

Yes, your inside is the key. Focus on your interior Presence while living each moment; for that is what is truly living and experiencing your life.

Talk to The One every moment. because it is a Universal Presence, and can perfectly respond to every situation you encounter and manage life gracefully. This *feeling of your Presence shall guide you* with blissful feelings in the moment.

Consider this: Who by THINKING fretful thoughts about any thing can make a balanced and appropriate choice regarding it?
Who can operate from a higher plane of Awareness when in worry?
Who can act in enlightenment when they have not yet entered therein?
And Who can move with confidence when standing in darkness?

The expression of Creative Power comes not from hoping but from knowing. It recedes away into un-confidence, in painful darkness, when fed by worry.
Power and confidence do not emerge from wishful thinking or uncertainty, but from the expression of our unified being which operates from the power of love. Therefore, listen now for the Secret of living life.

It is the power in love's attention that effects newness. Love is the Secret for transforming your present level of awareness, to illumination.

It begins in pointing your loving radiant attention toward
your Inner Being, where you find Freedom in Conscious Choice Making,
and it brings you purposeful power.

Attend to the feeling, knowing Living Presence in your Center with love
[your radiant Attention] and as you live each moment focused there,
all outside responsibilities that need taking care of shall in fact
be handled naturally. You will not have to worry over the little things,
and the necessities shall be taken care of with power.

"Your I AM Self—in whom you live and move and have your being" [C]
and "who dwells and walks and talks in you" [D]
"knows what things you have need of;
your I AM is not in the dark about your life."
It is divine pleasure to care for and feed you. [E]

You are a divine child, currently in an earthly expression
yet tenderly watched over.
You have too little faith in the Loving Power of your I AM
and so much faith in trouble and limitation.

What good can come from believing in trouble?
When attention is placed in fearful negative thinking,
it limits you and your life.

Expect the best. You're going to expect something anyway,
you might as well expect the best.

As a Child of Infinite Power and creativity, your attention is indeed
powerful. Your I AM has granted you, the "I" expressed—dominion
over your personal world, to manifest whatever you hold feelingly .. and
breathfully in consciousness.

It is ever radiating Divine Power, which flows through the LENS of your
Imagination and your Attention, to project your assumptions into being.
But it is you who directs your attention. Attention is the Secret Power
of love, but it is You that focuses your attention.

What is it that you hold in your mind? To what do you give your attention?
What images do you constantly hold of your life in your conscious
and subconscious centers?
What you see manifest as your personal life is the out-picturing of your
deeply held vision of yourself and your life, even if you don't believe it.

The having of a MIND and its focusing purposes are Your responsibility.
Take seriously your power.
Show prudence in choosing the beliefs you hold feelingly and the images
you hold continually of yourself in consciousness.

Remember, without an understanding of the Divine Law of love,
that love focuses your attention,
it is impossible to divinely pleasure the Divine One
who wishes you to consciously express his power effectively and lovingly.

For when we believe in love's radiant Attention,
love becomes visible as manifestation takes place.
Creation occurs as Love radiates Attention.

Just as confidence breeds more confidence, it is also true that when we
ascend into our Deep Self, our loving Creative Awareness,
Divine Love and Creative Power are expressed in this universe more often,
but they come through us, which creates Divine Pleasure, as the Divine
has another avenue of expression through which to work powerfully.

So you see, *your Divine I AM is always doing all it can do for you*, and
always will. God will not be doing something for you tomorrow that God
is not already doing for you today. *Divine Attention always shines on you.*
It is your attunement to the Divine Awareness deep within your
consciousness that creates your answered prayers, your success and joy.
It is by Altering your "held" self-image *to alignment* with your Divine Self,
that creates bliss.

When you ponder grace, grace occurs. The Divine experiences your bliss
and has continuous pleasure in your growth. God loves your
expanding Awareness .. especially your oneness with Him-Her.

It is Divine Power that rushes in to fill up the mold of your innermost
expanded assumptions and to *manifest your new understanding.*
If you spend time imagining and feeling your oneness with Divine Being,
then it is that Image that God shall manifest in the outer world.
It is your choice to focus on what you will.
It is your decision to hold onto the feelings that direct the flow
of your spirit, which in turn manifests for you according to your faith,
— that vision that you hold of yourself and your life.

Yet, there is a higher way to live and there is a path of grace. There is a
deeper friendship with the Divine. It comes by trusting your Infinite I AM
who loves you more than you love yourself, and letting It guide your day.
If you find that trying to govern your universe and life is exhausting,
then let go. Listen on the inside to your divine intuition, and obey it.

How? *Just do what seems the appropriate thing to do in each moment.*
And do whatever feels peaceful. Remember:
With inner quietness and confidence, you will always find strength. [W]

If you focus continuously on your **all-loving, all-providing
spiritual Vibration within, you will stay in touch with bliss.**
If you permeate your awareness with the graceful power of 'I Am One'
you will see Divine Grace manifest throughout your life by its guidance
of you. Any unpleasant conditions *manifested so far in your life* will drop
from you, since their existence lived only from your attention anyway.

Your staring at painful circumstances only keeps them with you.
Do not stare at your current negative situation. *Go within yourself daily*
to feel your oneness with Divine Being and obey God's leading from there.

Let your *heart-centered feelings* regarding each moment of the day
and each activity, be your GUIDE as to the appropriateness of your
thoughts and deeds.

If your heart remains peaceful before and during an activity,
instead of anxious, then you do well.
Trust that your life is actually being guided, and it will be.

Practice friendship with the Divine by listening to divine leadings.

'Acknowledge God in all your ways so God will direct your Paths in bliss.' [F]

'He shall keep him in perfect peace whose mind, thoughts and imagination are stayed on Him' [V]

Look within all day long as you look without,
and your Divine heart leading will direct your steps.

Follow your feelings moment-to-moment and let blissfulness be the guide.
By doing this, your heart shall rest in peaceful oneness, and your mind
shall be filled with lighted Awareness.
But it is .. a continual dedication. 36.

When you allow the Divine Individuality inside you to express,
what you allowed will expand you.
If you do not allow this within you to express, once again
you will TASTE the STING [the unconsciousness] of death. 70.

Splendorous Light Within

From our center will flow
self-sustaining Awareness that *feels* our life force
and our creative power *in motion;* and it
feels a Love, which fulfills itself by blessing All.

~ CHAPTER 5 ~

THE PATH OF ASCENSION:
Uniting Spirituality with the Outer Life

"If anyone thirst, let them come into Me and drink; For one who believes in Me out of his belly shall flow rivers of living water."
John 7:37

[From his center will flow self-sustaining awareness that feels his life force and creative power in motion; that feels a love that fulfills itself by blessing all]

Disciples then asked: "Do you think we should practice fasting, and how do you want us to pray, and… how should we distribute offerings, …and are their rules to be observed in eating?" 6.

He replied: "If you fast out of habit, or as a ritualistic duty, or in self-righteousness, you have missed the point of fasting, which is to willingly and cheerfully release any thing or any activity that prevents your attention from being focused on your divine guidance within. Focus on the essence of I AM—fasting from thought— then your mind will grow quiet, then, you can truly hear.

"If you attempt a food fast and fail to honor either the letter or the spirit of it, you will then judge yourself and will have created a SIN for yourself [literally a *"missing of the mark"*].
"Fasting from food provides dominion over your bodily appetites and passions, which is a necessary step and a profitable one to take.
It cleanses your bodily systems, which is also necessary.
But it is not an end in and of itself, and it does not create righteousness.
"However, fasting from old patterns and unconscious self-centered habits is true progress."

Regarding prayer, if you pray out loud to be seen of men, in a public show,
you may be judged by others as self-righteous
and public words would not be honored by your inner being, anyway.
Public words only "serve your ego," which exacts its own price,
feeling false rewards. [G]
Many words do not make a prayer. But just this—I AM—
can move mountains of trouble.

Prayer is not made with the lips
but with the utterings of the heart in its yearning for oneness.
True prayer is accomplished in inner privacy,
in the secret place of your soul and spirit. [H]
When you are in communion with your soul [your elevated consciousness]
and when you are one-with your spirit [the universal cosmic Breath],
you then rise above the ego state as you enter a Divine Silence to create.

In your divine center, you rest from your personality
and you are in touch with peace.   In prayer, you calm down.
Release your worries. They prevent entrance into your soul state.
Rest peacefully in prayer, in confident expectancy, knowing it is a
divine pleasure to give you the whole Consciousness.
True prayer creates a delightful integration between
your personality awareness and your breath.

In truth, the answer to prayer exists before the prayer is made,
and it is yours before you claim it.
Your desire is its herald, your vision its promise.
Effective prayer concludes with *confidence* [with resolution that is felt].
In powerful prayer, we "see" or "feel" the outcome of the prayer
inside our being, and this creates a joyfulness.
Then we feel that it is "already accomplished."
We realize the Divine Presence *has gone ahead us, to accomplish the purpose.*

It is when we feel that click of joyfulness.   But do not undo it all later on with anxiety, worrying over it. Your joy is the sign, and your peacefulness, marks its certainty.   When Divine Being feels inner peace and gratitude in you its power is released.   This is because your inner unification occurs.

You see, your Soul [*Divine Will*] unites with your Breath[*Cosmic Creativity*].
Then ever-Radiating power and ever-flowing divine substance move into
your inner vision [the joyfully nurtured interior event]
and its manifestation is brought out.

Create by becoming one-with your desire. It is a realization and a feeling.
Prayer is not about asking for something or saying "I want."
The result of prayer can only be *your wanting*.
Wanting is a state of lack—but gratitude is an experience of being whole.
You shall have whatever you really believe. Prayer sees and feels it NOW…
not then. Don't put it off. Everything is actually one with you already.
See it, feel it, claim it, smile. It is all here now in the invisible.
We make it visible by attracting it to us within.

You must create consciously if you wish to escape your past.
Prayer is about the present, not the future, Not Maybe but creativity Now.
It is divine joy to co-create with a conscious you;
unconscious creation can be painful.
You are a door from Heaven into this world of matter, into this
world of experiencing. You are the outlet for creation.
Desires arrive by coming 'through you'.
Know this, prayer is unlimited and effortless.
It can be offered up all the time. It is for quietly expressing gratitude in
every moment of the day. It is in every moment that your
divine **Father-Mother** [your soul and spirit] provide your life and breath,
your consciousness and creativity and all things in gracefulness.
So say "Thank you" at every turn, *everywhere* in any moment.

Now, when you give OFFERINGS from religious duty or outside pressure,
it is not from a heart of benevolence, understanding, or cheer.
So instead of receiving a blessing from giving, which is divine law,
a baptism of emotional pain is felt at being forced.
But when true giving occurs, the gift is given cheerfully
to your Deep Self—to God, *in the other person*.

And God is constantly replacing the gift and giving a hundredfold
to her children in return for their sharing with each other.

So give where it is needed, where the gift will be felt, giving with personal
attention, for your Divine "I" loves the thoughtfulness of this strategy.

And wherever you go, whenever you travel, and hospitality is offered,
eat what is set before you and aspire to love. Do not argue over food.
It is not what goes into your mouth that defiles you,
but what comes out of your mouth in painful creativity.
Help others in whatever way you can. Stretch forth your hands
and heal any sickness among them with your warmth.
Speak your words in loving kindness, for their pain may be great. 14.

Grapes are not gathered from thorn bushes, and figs are not picked
from thistles. Just so, a good man brings forth excellence from his heart.
But an un-united man, living backwards, in shadows and selfishness
brings forth condemnation and pain from his ego nature,
speaking negativity when he communicates himself. 45.

Therefore, do not practice lying about yourself or others.
Speaking the truth energizes your spiritual growth
and reinforces your ability to focus the light of awareness,
which discerns between human perception and truth.

Your soul always knows the truth. It is everywhere. Rely on that.
Lying is injurious, most especially to the one who lies.
Speaking truthfully allows you to make positive accomplishments in rising
above the worldly ego nature, which is all the time rehearsing deception.

When you stand in truth, you "face the sun" and you allow light
[true Awareness] to clean you of shadow areas in the ego persona;
**those mental and behavioral habit patterns that are constantly seeking
reinforcement and repeated validation, that consistently
make slaves of the children of earth**, who are under their dark and
heavy burden. Arise and throw off the bonds of deception and "sleep,"
which maintain that stagnating, primitive ego facade.

Take the first conscious step. It is all important. **Wake up with Intentions.**
Because *the first step of your ascension* toward Self [*toward your interior life*]
is the death knell for the old life [*that external focus on ego appetites*].

Don't do things to others or yourself, OF Which you disapprove,
because it breaks down your centeredness, and causes contradictions
within yourself .. that have to be cleaned out later.
Don't agitate your consciousness *Practicing deceit*, but let it soar with
integrity. Your participating in deceitfulness only pulls it into Your life
(for you to deal with). Doing things of which you disapprove only adds to
your burden, and causes you to use universal and personal energy painfully.
Follow the admonition:
Don't do what you want ...then you can do what you like. [I]

The fact ever remains, in a universe founded on truth, light, and
Omnipresent Consciousness, everything done in secret, for good or ill,
will be shouted from the HOUSE TOPS
[*will be revealed by and In your Face, Words and Person*a].
Everything hidden will be revealed, and nothing covered
will remain undiscovered. For as it is within, so shall it be without. 6.

It is a blessing when a destructive ego-appetite is consumed by one's soul,
because its transformation into spirituality provides a new sense of
dominion that is unsurpassed on the path of personal growth.
Even the pleasure of one's cherished talents do not compare to the pleasure
of feeling this dominion. But it is abject sorrow when the awareness of soul
is consumed by one's uncontrolled appetites, because then, non-awareness
and inner pain, will sadly, be continuously experienced .. and feelings
of worthlessness and hopelessness can run rampant within one's being. 7.

So look to the *Living Consciousness within*, that formed your body-temple,
beats your heart, breathes your breath, and receive help, rising into dominion.
Do this as long as you live, lest you die in this world "under the thumb"
of ego patterns, then start searching for him inside Eternity,
at the outset feeling failure. 59.

Then they said: "Well come master, and let us pray today and fast".
Jesus said: "You say that as if there were a particular sin to be removed.
I AM always fasting from the world system,
and I AM in constant communion and prayer with my 'I AM I' within,
— listening to its leadings.   It is absolute bliss to do so".
You see, if one has lost touch with one's spiritual I AM — that heavenly bridegroom to one's earthly persona — then indeed let one FAST from ego patterns, for extended periods of time if necessary, in the wilderness of solitude, and let one PRAY powerfully, to recollect one's True self. 104.

Some disciples asked him:
"Is circumcision a truly needful or *righteous* thing to do?"
He replied: "If it were useful toward your transformation out of ego,
the Divine Mind that formed you would have circumcised you from birth.
However, the circumcision of ego-impulses and down-pulling habits
has always been beneficial and always will be.
The ***preserving and focusing of sexual energy is the real meaning of circumcision***; take up that discipline "of preserving-focusing sexual energy," if you desire powerful growth".
That energy is awesome for transformation, used properly. 53.

I say unto you *pitiful is the body-personality sustained solely by food and drink without the nourishment of the soul,* and its now-moment guidance.
Sad is the soul whose body remains non-integrated with its wholeness, whose aspects remain *half..in sensory pleasure seeking*, and not Whole. 87.

Then he said: "Honor the Divine Life within you,
which was unified before you became two weakened halves.
Because if you follow my example and hear my words,
truth will spontaneously rise up within you, serving your Awareness,
to make you Whole again.
This spontaneous and beneficial interior Assistance will bless and surprise you to no end. You will feel like a favorite child,
and you will smile incessantly."

There are five WAYS [five yogas or life systems] on the spiritual path
for one to practice everyday. They are: ***Loving service*** —
Faithfulness in word and deed — ***Knowledge*** gathering —
Discipline for breathing, mental cleanliness and *action for conscious evolution* and finally, ***Worshipping*** [going joyfully within to silently listen and commune with your divine Soul-Mind].

Practicing these five activities raises your desires above self-centeredness
and leads you away from sleep-inducing ego habits.
They place your focus onto truly living and onto your inner beingness,
as opposed to habitual patterns and the beliefs of the outer world.
And in neither the 'summer or winter' of your life
will these activities lose their fruit of transformational effectiveness.

For the person who practices all of them, a special nourishment shall be
bestowed. They will feel self-sustaining Divine Life moving
within them each moment, and they shall not TASTE death
[*make life-transition unconsciously*]. And they will avoid assigning to
themselves another life of confusion [in non-awareness] in which
struggling to Awaken to our true Identity, occurs all over again. 19.

Why do people wash the outside of their life, washing their external body
and affairs, and forget about cleansing their inside with Silence?
For the purity of mind and heart is the true purity,
and it is cleansed in the silence of solitude.

Do they not realize that the outside of their life is soiled because of the
uncleanness and distracting noise of their mental world?
Do they not know their mind is soiled by participating
in worldly activities? 89.

We see the small character flaw within our brother's persona,
but we do not see the massive personal flaw within our own.
Once we have overcome our weaknesses and begun to see our true Self,
we can help our brother see his. 26.

Remember, *when the blind lead the blind, they fall together* in the ditch. 34.

One's spiritual persona is not honored in public.
A Prophet is Not honored among his friends.
Just as physicians do not generally have good friends who are
willing patients, one's spiritual Identity is not taken seriously. 31.

Do not give the sacred to dogs and do not speak your truth to those
who care not for it or who will mock you,
for it's casting what is precious to the dung heap.
Just as you would not *cast pearls before swine*, for they would destroy them,
do not place your spiritual energy or precious truth out into the public eye
of skepticism and ridicule, to those who are uninterested and undeserving,
for you could be the one injured. 93.

Love your neighbor as your own soul
[for your soul is one with all neighbors]
and cherish him as your most beloved treasure. 25.

Love your neighbor as your own soul
and cherish him as your most beloved treasure.

You are in the Divine Presence wherever you are;
whether you're in the desert, the sea,
or at the gates of the grave...even there,
your Christ Self shall hold you.

~ CHAPTER 6 ~
LIVING AMID THE CHALLENGES AND TESTS

*"There is one body and one breath,
one Lord and one faith, one baptism, one God and Father of all,
who is above all, through all, and in you all."* Eph. 4:4-6

"I and the Father are one."
John 10:30

Blessed are the POOR
[*blessed are people Not driven to manifest the values of this world-system
in their life's heart-space — like those always wanting more;
operating from an empty sense.. of ego-power and pride*].
These will not be burdened with the self-made troubles
of unconscious creation in their life.
They shall have a rich and peaceful heart, being fulfilled in their
awareness of Soul, which delivers its loving influence continually,
all the way out to their physical life and daily awareness. 54.

Blessed are the ones who have come to understand suffering,
for it appears to be a mystery.
They learn not to rely on the outer world or its comforts,
for their peace and consolation.
They truly discover the warmth and reliability of meditating upon
their Inner Being and upon the truth:
'Consciousness is expressing my Awareness from deep inside myself' 58.

Count it a blessing if people persecute or hate you, and truly, if you're
beaten, for they assist you, teaching you not to look for your good in
the outside life. Actually, they eliminate only the pride of the human
personality when they torment you. But the purity of your Eternal Self
within, remains and shines through. 68.

Blessed are those who have suffered from being persecuted in their heart [where their I AM Presence is] Who feels with them and comforts them, in their solitude; And who,
because of this shared experience, is felt by them.
Blessed are the hungry for that soul guidance within;
for if they seek after it, they shall be filled and satisfied
and will ascend above the mundane weaknesses of the ego. 69.

When your teachers talk about the arrival of *the Kingdom*
[*the consciousness of bliss and power*] and if they say it is an external event —
and that it will descend from the sky, you will know this is untrue, because, if it was an external event, then the birds in the sky would arrive in heaven before you, the Divine Child, would arrive.

If your teachers falsely claim this Kingdom is off in the future, you will know this is untrue because then, your descendants would arrive *before you*. These common teachings are error, because Now is the acceptable time, Now is the day of salvation, not then [K]
The truth is Now is the only time we have, and Here is all there is.

The Kingdom of God is in Power. It produces a sound mind,
and it is for your edification now. Remember, it was said,
"*The Kingdom of Heaven* [the Expansive Awareness] *is at hand.*" [L]
It is because it is here, Now, right where you are.
It is inside your own being, for it is your life.

The Kingdom of God [Divine Domicile] is within you. [M]
It is in your very PRESENCE. [C]
It is the living, breathing, feeling, Creative Consciousness being you —
guiding you, shining out from you, and living you. [D]

You are one breath with God. There is no outside to Divine Being. This Divine Essence is also without you, omnipresently existing everywhere, in everything. [R]

You are in the Divine Presence wherever you are;
whether you are in the desert, the sea, "the Hell of human thinking"
or at the gates of the GRAVE;
even there, your Christ Self shall hold you [the earthly persona].   [N]
But it is no farther away than your own consciousness and breath,
for you are The One. When you know your Self, YOU will be known.
You will know that you are an expression of your invisible I AM —
that you are a PORTAL between Heaven and Earth. [S]
You will know, as I do, that I AM is the DOOR, I AM is the truth,
I AM is the life, and I AM is the WAY to the great I AM I. [O]

This mystery of *God's divine oneness with us,* is the secret.
For what could God express from, but His/Her one Infinite beingness.
There is not God, and something else. There is only God.
So you see, this is why I speak not of myself.
The words I speak are not my own.
The Divine Presence within me, He speaks and He performs the works,
and my I AM sends me and I obey. [P]
So if you do not know your Self, you are in poverty and you are poverty.
If however you do know, you shall be a power-point for The All,
and you shall source healing. 3.

Show me THE STONE [the spiritual Truth]
which the religious leaders rejected,
and I will show you, the CORNER STONE [Primary Truth]
of our Divine teaching and you will see that it is a spiritual Identity
within humanity... that is our very life.
You will then know that our Identity of Light is our permanent Self!

Our Identity, is a Divine Light Child. It is the I AM individualized as "I"
but this "I" is one with an Infinite "I AM" which inhabits everything,
including our being.
This Infinite One is beyond your human mind, in back of mentation.
It precedes your thoughts, judgments, emotions, and rationalization.

This Living One is discovered in your Breath and in Consciousness itself;
for It actually envelopes, permeates, and interpenetrates our human form,
our life, and our ego-brain, living in the past, with which we contend so
often [and on which we needlessly place so much of our daily attention].

In fact, this Divine One inhabits our entire universe –
here, there, every where .. and in past, present, and future.
God's Mind holds the essential reality every where ... in everything:
in you, as you, and always in every way, and in every where.

This is your destination.
You must find this essence of Self to know your bliss.
To find that Center of consciousness within your Self, pause, rest,
and start feeling.

Find that Movement and Rest ... every moment as you breathe.
It is your Original State and it is your initial, primary stage of being. 66.

CHAPTER 6 ~ *Living Amid the Challenges*

This is your Destination.
You must find this *essence of Self*
to know your Bliss.

Splendorous Light Within

You came from Light — Living Awareness,
and you are Light — Conscious Divine Awareness,
and to this Light, you shall return.

~ Chapter 7 ~

Reunification: Your Discipline and Destination

*"You shall know the truth, and the truth
shall make you free."*   ~John 8:32

His disciples asked him: "Tell us how our end will be?"
Jesus said: "Do you really understand your origin, that you can now
ask about your end?
Our end is the same as our beginning. They're both found in God's Light.
You came from Light — Living Awareness,
and you are Light — Conscious Divine Awareness,
and to this Light you shall return."

Blessed are the ones who know their beginning,
for this is their permanent Home, and they shall not TASTE death.
Not TASTING death means not making transition in a "sleeping" state
and experiencing it as many do, unconsciously, without conscious consent.
Many are unaware and are unwillingly Carried obliviously by the 'current'
of their old awareness and their old belief system..
to a dimension where similarly unaware and like-minded souls congregate.

In this way, by practicing principles that foster Divine Awareness,
one will not fall under the power of one's former non-awareness during
life transition, but will go to the LIGHT fully conscious of the process,
and the destination. 18.

An OLD MAN [*the ego persona in one*] heavily burdened with beliefs
about separateness from God, will not hesitate to ask a NEW CHILD
of Divine Awareness – only seven days old and freshly REBORN, about
the wondrous Presence emanating *in him*…and how he happened on it.
Then that "Old Man" shall find the same Place within his own being,
he too will transform, and There he too shall Live.

Many who appear in "first place" in this world shall transcend last;
and many who have appeared to "win the prize" here…
have actually lived in pain and sorrow [*residing daily in their ego mind*]
and have experienced separation from true Love, in their Soul
and perhaps shall be the last to see the Divine One in their Center.
For why should they seek their Center when it has always been confused
with painful human thinking and discontent?

But one day, they too will discern the difference between
the Love of and In soul… and the hell of ego-mentation [inner pain].
So eventually, all individuals, will see the Truth of our being,
and ALL will be united within their Infinite Divine Presence. 4.

Then he put forth a question: Consider this:
If the bodily flesh came here to serve the breath, that would be a mystery;
but if the breath came here to serve the body, that would be a miracle.
Do you know why such wealth makes its home in such "apparent" poverty?
If you do, then you know that Individuality and Embodiment are the
Divine Intent; and that the maturity gained through embodiment,
regarding mercy, with its evolved and mature wisdom,
are the benefits of incorporating consciousness within a body.

Also, the deep appreciation that our earthly experience provides to us
regarding bliss, when it is juxtaposed to the Painful Grace,
which comes from human suffering,
makes one realize that Individual Embodiment, is The Divine Way
of sharing with us, the Greatest, richest, most salient insights on being. 29.

No individual Living the Truth, *high* in the MOUNTAINS of Pure
Consciousness [*within his true Identity*] can fall; nor can he conceal himself.
For when one *attains unification* with the Living Spirit [*the conscious Breath*]
and realizes the Wholeness and Power of operating from one's
Unified Being, one is not able to hide that fact.
However, remain MEEK [teachable] and HUMBLE [wisely allowing]
so that Awareness *will arrive.* 32.

Then he said: Whatever you understand in Full Awareness, *knowing it within and manifesting it without as well,* you may teach "with your Mouth" to the truth-seeking children; and as The Mouthpiece of I AM, you will bring them new Awareness.

For as no one lights a lamp in order to place it UNDER a Basket, neither will The Divine enlighten an individual to keep them shut up or keep them away from the world.
They are put on a "stand" [in position] to let their INNER LIGHT shine so that all who ENTER or DEPART this world, may see and know that LIGHT and *Also* have the opportunity to experience true Awareness. 33.

If you understand that your origin comes from Infinite Divine Light, *where everything originates,* then what is hidden will be known by you, and you shall know that you Are, and that you ever *Will be.* 5.

When you look into mirrors, or see your image in a picture, you are interested in your image.
But when your *Mind's Eye beholds your personally held* MENTAL IMAGES constantly rising before you, neither subsiding nor approaching, what will you do with them?

These private thoughts endlessly hover around our consciousness. They haunt the mind, arising from one's personal hell of "thought taking," anxiety, or worry. They are bolstered by FEARS and NIGHTMARES, and by a fretful, negative Imagination.

How long can you withstand the pressure of this inner pain?
When will it all be enough?
Why will you not surrender the Mind's focus back to the I AM—the blissful place—instead of in anxious mentation?
Continual inner communion is what I speak of.
I AM Awareness is where your life is *peacefully maintained* and truly utilized.
Take no anxious thought for "not now – not here thinking".
Sufficient unto today are the adversities thereof.

Therefore, let him who is willing listen now and act appropriately!
Remain in the present moment—in pure I AM awareness, always just here and right now. Let go of all yesterdays and their sorrows, they are gone.
Let go of your tomorrows, which are not yet in awareness.
Living today in wonder—in the now-moment—creates blissful tomorrows.
Count your blessings. Enjoy and be thankful for all that belongs to this moment, whatever it is, and be enthusiastically involved in that activity.

Let go of control. Stop trying to run or 'pattern' this life after mental fixations and egotistical agendas.
Stop the endless criticism of yourself and others, even in your mind.
Let everyone be… especially yourself.

Let peace flow between you and others, and between your thoughts.
The I AM will provide whatever you need to learn from experience.
You are the judge of no one, so let judging go away from you.
And be gentle on yourself.
However, give yourself some disciplines to refine your nature.
As you do, your refinements will become you;
they will *give birth to new growth,* ever new expansion, and new disciplines.

Your greatest endeavor is in Loving yourself—and others—through loving expansiveness. You actually Assist others on their life paths, and your own as well, by taking charge of pointless appetites, which make others stumble as your lives touch.

Your Expansive Kindness, however, inspires other people's lives with a love from Above.
When your love goes out to others, it returns again to you a hundred fold, becoming the Grace to you that it was to them.

In doing these things you become a clear LENS and a clean VESSEL through which the Original Being may work the wonders
of the Infinite One … in you. 84.

There are many at the threshold of their I AM awareness, but not realizing
how to enter; yet only the 'Solitary Ones' enter into this bliss, entering
without an agenda of "me too." Only those who have *united* their
soul, breath, and body into a singleness of purpose—whose
Intention, Attention, Action are united in surrendering the "*me too ego*"
(toward rejoining the Oneness)—
will reunite with the Living One, within themselves consciously.

These shall enter the BRIDAL CHAMBER
[the divine temple/Consciousness].
These shall join together the NEW HEAVEN [the new spiritual Awareness]
with the NEW EARTH [the newly developed Body] within their life,
and shall become the embodiment of divine peace,
[becoming the "Jerusalem" consciousness in their Individuality].

This means your LIGHT Consciousness *is wed to the earthly temple;* that is,
the BRIDE GROOM [your Christ Mind] takes residence with the BRIDE
[*your divine Breath-Breathing*] which gives birth to the Child of Light
and its life within your earthly form, as you are then "born from Above,"
and you become the "Son of Man" who understands this truth.
So do not become a person known for their much 'talking'
who is always at the door of Heaven, yelling "Let me in,"
when there is room for only *The One*.

When will you be done believing in your separation from Divine Being,
as if there is you and It?
Hear plainly, Children of the Divine:
Divine Consciousness is your consciousness.
Divine Breath is your breath.
The Divine Heart beats your heart.
The entire life of our divinity is One life—in a Oneness,
and it is expressed in infinite variety.

There is no one else, besides God, anywhere. 75.

Splendorous Light Within

CHAPTER 7 ~ *Reunification: Your Destination*

Just as sun rays awaken the earth in the morning from its cool darkness, so will that moment be in you, which reunites Light and shadow, Spirit and flesh...and the *'I AM'* to the *'I'* within.

~ Chapter 8 ~

The Kingdom of Heaven:
Our Ever-Expanding Expansive Awareness

"Be you transformed by the renewing of your mind."
Romans 12:2

Disciples challenged: "So tell us what the Kingdom of Heaven is like."
Jesus responded by teaching them the symbols of the Kingdom:
The expansive Divine Awareness grows within your heart
just as the incredibly small MUSTARD SEED grows in a GARDEN.
Although it is the smallest of garden seeds, it eventually becomes
the largest, most expansive life in the GARDEN [of your heart],
so that all the BIRDS of the AIR [your intuitional spiritual thoughts]
will make their home in your now-moment Awareness, giving you bliss.

It may appear that spirituality can be crowded out of your awareness
by other PLANTS and WEEDS
[worldly thoughts, dogma, misinformation],
but it grows beyond them, and surpasses in size, stature, and life force.

Then all the activity of your heart is overshadowed and blessed
by the expansive Life Force of your purest inner Awareness,
which will transform the nature of everything within and around you,
providing an inexplicable constant cheer. 20.

Any path, system, philosophy, or endeavor conjured by the human ego
does not have inherent life in it; so if it is not tethered in the Truth that we
are one-with Divine Being, it will be torn at its roots and inevitably die. 40.

However, when a Spiritual Messenger comes into the world,
he spends his life planting spiritual SEEDS [words/ideas] that have a
deep spiritual root and feeds all our hearts with the spiritual life
of our oneness with God, which is eternal.

The SOWER casts his words across the **Ground** of many listeners' hearts.
A few words fall upon the ROADWAY where busy people and bystanders
listen a moment but, disinterested, continue their daily affairs, and forget
the words quickly. Other words fall upon hearts who, though they listen,
are filled with a love of money and lusts of the world, placing their
attention on pursuits that do not nurture the new words that have fallen.
Still other words fall upon GOOD SOIL [open receptive hearts] where the
words are like LEAVENING *[catalyzing* 'spiritual seeds'] and they expand
the listeners' awareness of their I AM Life Force, allowing divine experience
and knowing, true peace, and unconditional love to flourish. 9.

Awaiting the full bloom of this individualized Expansive Divine Awareness
is analogous to a full SEASON through which a FARMER [God] waits,
because God has sown GOOD SEED of truth in the FIELD of your heart.
Yet among the Words of Life, the 'world' sows WEEDS in our Heart-SOIL
  [negative identifications in our consciousness; such as painful
  self-images, desires for money and worldly things, laziness, jealousy,
  greed, gluttony, violence].
Such addictive patterns and habitual weaknesses make humanity maintain
its attention on the body, the personality, the world, and on satisfying
temporary appetites, *instead of on the Life of the Inner Self, the truth & inner*
divine power. It is as if the world is trying to make us forget seeking our
pure Awareness and to stop attending to our soul, wherein,
we find our Permanence.

But the FARMER [Infinite Being] knowing the strength of His seed,
that it would not be choked out by the WEEDS, but would grow beyond
the weeds, said, do not worry over these WEEDS
[the erroneous beliefs in their mind]. We will not upset the progress
of new spiritual growth already present in their awareness.

On HARVEST DAY
[on the day they transcend their ego identity, in the FIRE of the Breath]
they will enter into EXPANSIVE AWARENESS instead,
and our good SEEDS will Expand, and the WEEDS [old belief systems]
will be uprooted and burned in the FIRE of realization.
So, when the FIRE in consciousness comes, the root causes of the ego life
[those misidentifications and mistaken beliefs about Identity]

will be cleansed out of this experience.
Therefore, look for and be prepared for your Spiritual Fire
[*in your spiritual Breathing*].
It will arrive for every person at his own divinely appointed time.
It will be a day like any other, except that moment will be like dawn.

Just as sun rays awaken the earth in the morning from its cool darkness,
so will that moment be In You — which reunites Light and shadow,
Spirit and flesh, and the " I AM " to the " I " – within your individuality;
On that day your inhale and your exhale shall be as one, and the power
of the Fire Breath shall transform your earthly body to a Light Body —
a body not restrained by earth and its gravity.
On a day when there is marrying and playing, and working and eating,
IT shall come; in the hour when *personal disconnected thought-taking* ceases.

And at a time, when you see within your heart, a vision of your True Being,
the transformation will occur in you, and the Child of Light
will take its place in you.
Then you cease from being '*MAN whose breath is in his nostrils*'.
You will cease this fruitless scheming and fearful mentations.
You will finally rest within your Divine I AM
as your Christed Awareness permanently replaces this limited mentality.
This removes "the veil" from True Insight and you *see into The All,*
And it will unravel the mysteries and purposes of all things. 57.

Maintaining your conscious spiritual Awareness requires the care and
vigilance that a SHEPHERD [*one who has a conscious evolutionary path*]
has for his one-hundred SHEEP [for his life's spiritual priorities].
The person who has a spiritual path tries to live consciously, and on
purpose, so he exercises disciplines over mind and body in order to create a
good life. However, among most people [*shepherds*] those with a conscious
spiritual path the most important dedication [*sheep*] has been left behind
and is missing. It is the true Idea of real living, that of witnessing the Christ
Mind operate one's life. This is most often missing from human awareness,
even from successful human awareness, even from rich people who enjoy
earthly abundance; because normally, the ego wants to run our life,
fulfilling its own agendas, despite our spiritual longings.

So the WISE SHEPHERD [disciple] does not focus on the 99 things of his
life so that he may find his Christ Identity ... and he will do that, until he
finds it. After all his searching efforts, when he finds his Authentic Self, he
will say, "I love you, my Christ Awareness, more than the 99 other things
of my life [*more than religions, possessions, philosophies, careers, wealth, fame*].

With everything in proper priority — with our Christ Consciousness in
ascendance, *we can attend to all of life's matters* and better than before. 107.

The Expansive Awareness within your heart SERVES you like a WOMAN
[*like your Holy Spirit's nurturing guidance*]
who adds LEAVEN *[transformative awareness]*
to her BREAD DOUGH [to her child of earth]
so as to BAKE a hearty large LOAF [a powerful child of God]
creating a loving, wise, and powerful Child of Light. *If you understand
about this inner Breath assistance,* then receive this *interior help* and grow. 96

Faithfully focusing daily Attention on your spiritual Self cleanses your
interior being and empowers you for your journey Home.
It has to do with maintaining a true focus.
It is likened to a WOMAN [*our Holy Breath's nurturing Wisdom*]
who is carrying a JAR full of FLOUR MEAL on a long JOURNEY,
[*like our inner Spirituality carrying an ego full of worldly concerns
 while walking through the human life experience*].

When the JAR HANDLE 'breaks,' something happens.
The FLOUR MEAL streams out BEHIND and is left on the ROADSIDE
[*when the ego's controlling grip is broken through our letting go of old
identifications, old fears, and old judgments regarding our self and our life*].
Then we are freed of the weight of these energy-draining concerns.

Now, because our Attention is turned AWAY from the past and its
negativity, our spirit's creative capacity does not continue producing
unpleasant manifestations. By and by, it is not noticed that the Jar's
WEIGHT *[the ego's burden]* becomes LIGHTER
[*our tendency not to notice our own progress*].

However, upon arriving HOME
[*to the Christ Realization that "my Father and I are one"*]
that Consciousness is one-with Expression.
Then we set down the JAR
[we *completely surrender the ego identification*] and find, it is empty. 97.

Acquiring the expansive spiritual Awareness is analogous to a merchant
who discovers that a truly rare and priceless PEARL
[*our pure interior Energy*] is available for his creative use.
So important is this pearl to him that he SELLS all his POSSESSIONS
[*ceases the practice of scheming and thought-taking in the ego*]
then he goes and BUYS the PEARL
 [lives by feeling and developing the Spiritual Energy of his Heart Center,
 rather than relying upon the continuous thought life in his mind,
 and that true heart focus becomes his life's power].
Seek like him, that TREASURE within your awareness of heart,
which does not fade, nor crack, nor depreciate like material wealth.
Find true riches in the permanent I AM Consciousness within your
Deep Self, where no moths or worms can enter to consume or corrupt. 76.

Achieving the Expansive Divine Awareness requires personal fortitude and
persistence. Because a person must eradicate the ego's imbedded mental
patterns and personality habits that hide our pure Awareness from view.
But this eradication of ego patterns is accomplished by looking to our
inner Fire to burn these patterns out of our daily life.

Your Fortitude and Persistence is focused inward. This inner focus will do
the eradicating of our ego patterns. The small will-power of the ego mind,
when it's directed toward ending its own habits, *is not where we find the
power to transcend.* That power is found in our Divine Soul.
So this person practices utilizing incisive discernment into his own nature,
to discover its *currents and shadows, to find his weaknesses and temptations.*
He brings all his powers of focus into the Home of *his divine Breath
awareness,* to know as much about himself as he does about his profession.
This way he can live *each moment freely without being run*
by his ego's agenda.

He practices employing a decisive WILL to focus his Attention on
Divine Being within, And in doing so will delete his ego's ingrained habits
one by one, as they are observed in consciousness.
He does this to develop excellence in his life—striking DEATH BLOWS
to his old habits and old identifications; such as pessimism, fear, and
laziness; which only serve as road blocks to transformation.
Then one day, his ego identification is simply eliminated altogether. 98.

The HIDDEN yet ever-present nature of our inner I AM
is similar to a man who is ignorant of a TREASURE [of Divine Being]
hidden in his FIELD [*hidden in his transpersonal heart-level awareness*].
When he dies, his son INHERITS this same Lack of spiritual awareness,
so that he too is unaware of the TREASURE within and, not knowing better,
SELLS the FIELD [pursues money and worldly things].

However, the BUYER comes [*the one on a Spiritual Path arrives*]
and while working continuously on daily transformations,
discovers the TREASURE *[the Lighted Beingness within himself
　　　　　　　　　giving explosive power to his spiritual endeavor]*
and he esteems IT above everything worldly, and allows it to express,
and IT will benefit many,
and he himself receives More from its daily Increase. 109.

Having prepared a banquet, Divine Being sent his SERVANT
[the soul's voice of guidance into the awareness of humanity]
and he summoned the invited GUESTS — the most Aware leaders
of humanity's culture. So the servant went to them and reminded them
of their invitations to the divine BANQUET
[*to the inner heavenly Consciousness*].

Well-placed people often respond to their Spiritual Conscience like this:
"*I have to advise some merchants in my debt, who are visiting me;
I cannot come.*" Others say: "*I have bought a house and I must care for it.
I have no time.*" Others reply: "*I'm sorry but my friend is getting married,
and I must organize a celebration dinner.
I'm too busy for spiritual disciplines.*"

Still others respond to their Intuitive Spiritual Guidance with the excuse:
"*I just bought a business and I must collect accounts payable today that are very important.*"

The Divine Servant [our soul's voice] comes back to our Divine Life Force *unrequited*, reporting that the guests are not coming and are too busy with worldly responsibilities to spend time with their God.

So Divine Being responds to its Soul Desire, saying:
"*Then go into the streets and byways and make yourself known to the common folk and invite them.. to partake of their Divine Consciousness* [they HAVE the time]; *for they will lead well-placed people into the Consciousness of bliss and power. The weak shall lead the powerful, the poor will guide the rich, the dumb will confound the mighty, and a Christ Child in their Center shall lead them all into the dominion of a divinely powerful life, in joyful liberty.*"

People who pursue money, things, and worldly power do not enter the Consciousness of their Divine Interior; for they are too busy to come in and sup with their Divine Mind. They are too pleased with their earthly affairs to know Me, or to find true joy, liberating light, or the true power of Divine Love in their lives. 64.

A rich man with a great fortune decided to expand his wealth even more by investing and selling and investing again; that he might fill his bank account to overflowing with money and assets. He did it to feel secure and accomplished, and to gain even more recognition. However, that very night he died in "monetary darkness" – *poverty stricken in spirit.*

Let him who under stands, fulfill his Divine Purpose of knowing God while he IN the world. 63.

One who is rich in this world attains many material things and can become a "king"; but one who is powerful within needs nothing this world offers, and joyfully transcends it — in spiritual awareness. 81.

If you have monetary wealth, do not lend it out at interest
but give it to them who will not need to repay it. 95.

Let it be a gift, given cheerfully and without mindfulness of virtue. (X)

He who has found the world and its riches should remove himself
from worldly activities and pursuits, to find his Original Divine Identity
and his real purpose in the world.
If you have money, use the opportunity it provides,
to find and know your true Self.

How much simpler can it be? Use the opportunity that money provides
to find your Divine Beingness; and when you do,
you then have the monetary power to do real good. 110.

Disciples asked: "So, Master, when will the rest for the dead begin?
And when will the New World appear?"
He answered: "The Divine Interior Sanctuary that you're expecting
is already here, although you do not recognize it.

The Divine Kingdom is spread out all around you right now.
You are already in it. You live in Divine Mind.
You are never alone, and you are enveloped in love.

Love is at the center of all things.
The Divine Kingdom of YOUR God is WITHIN you.
Rest in that knowledge as you live and breathe." 51.

Love is at the center of all things.
The Divine Kingdom of Your God is Within you.
Rest in that knowledge as you live and breathe.

Now, the day you discover your true light,
your current idea of spirituality will PASS AWAY
behind you, feeling like another life or a dream.

~ CHAPTER 9 ~

LIVING DAILY
THE LIFE OF TRANSFORMATION

"I baptize you with water, but he that comes after me is mightier than I and he shall baptize you with the Holy Breath and Fire." [lightened Inner purification]." –John the Baptist, Matthew 3:11

Jesus said: "I shall destroy this HOUSE
[this present Consciousness-Temple].
I will leave it behind and nobody will be able to restore it.
Although I – *the Christ*—to teach you about the power of pure Awareness – will raise it up again,

I can pick it up or lay it down, for I express this earthly image
and I have power over what is called life and death."   71.

His disciples asked him: "Tell us about the place where you live,
for we will seek for it if you teach us how."
Jesus said: "Let him who understands this Mystery, act on it every day:

There is the light of the Divine One within us.
 It is a Divine Awareness in our center, which guides our daily living.
It is where we experience wisdom, joy, peace, love, and power.
These qualities shine from one who daily immerses himself meditatively
in this inner Living Awareness, and he naturally shares this loving light,
impartially, with everyone in his world.
"If he does not share his interior light, there is darkness out here
in his world.
For darkness is an external focus in '*living* the world-system';
But Awareness is attending to .. and communing with his inner light.

Our purpose then is to BRING LIGHT [bring healing Awareness]
to DARKNESS [to human confusion and pain]."   24.

Now, the day you discover your true light [*your Divine Awareness within*]
your current idea of spirituality will PASS AWAY behind you,
feeling like another life or a dream. Your present belief systems and
old identifications will also pass away behind you.
Your unenlightened ego-persona will no longer dominate, as you've
removed attention from it ... and your rediscovered one true Self
will no longer pass through the sleepy transition of "death".

You now remember, that once when you practiced good habits —
when you practiced spiritual disciplines to enter your I AM Self —
it was you, [the one who believed in separation]
that put forth effort and allowed an unfolding expression of good works.

But when you reenter your Divine Light, and your expansive Awareness,
who do you suppose will be the ACTOR then, who will be the DOER,
and WHO will be doing the allowing?
Will it be the ego self, feeling separate, and alone — burdened with
the emptiness of the past…? Or will it be your Divine Beingness
acting from the Loving Power of the Present Moment?

In the beginning, when you were one-with "I AM I," you became "two"
by falling "asleep" and you dreamed of a "separation" from your
Divine Identity, believing the God Life Force to be someplace else,
other than in you, *as* your body and soul.

You dreamed that EARTH was separate from HEAVEN, and you focused
on the outer world's shadows and circumstances and dreamed of death
rather than knowing the power, present within your being.

But now that you are "two" [in a divided consciousness of half-ness],
how shall you return to The One, The Only, The Whole?
How can you rejoin what you never separated from,
or come back again to what you never left?

To awaken from your dream of exile, you must reorient your Awareness
of Self, by seeing your flesh as the *outside* of your breath,
and, unifying your divine impulses with your human actions.

CHAPTER 9 ~ *Life of Transformation*

Let your mind be the servant of your SOUL [your pure Intentions]
and let loving kindness replace ego's self-centeredness
[by continuously gazing within].
Listen to and touch the Divine Consciousness in your center of being
moment to moment, and obey the guidance that you receive there.
Listen.
You marvel at the things I do and the words I say, but marvel not.
The works I do and the words I say are from the "I AM I."
The words I hear the I AM say within, these I say;
and the works I see this Divine One do within, these are what I do.
You see, it is only a matter of attention and obedience. 11.

Then Jesus said: From ADAM
[our first 'governing' stage in the divisive "I am this body" belief]
to JOHN The BAPTIST [our final stage in this divided belief]
at no time has there been any phase in human experience,
nor any incarnation in this unawakened human condition,
which was more evolved than the Awareness *embodied in John the Baptist;*
for even his name means "from death into Divine Grace."

This Awareness, [personified as John] signifies our impending rebirth
into true Awareness. As this state, *precedes* the Awareness that the
Divine Life Force Is our human life force. So this **old awareness,**
[this belief in perfecting our humanity with '*human Will*']
eventually fades away. Even so, this '*perfecting*' *stage,*
symbolized as John the Baptist, remains unexpressive of the truth that
the Divine Presence, is our human presence.

So after this stage exhaustedly transpires, soon enough,
we Rise to the higher level of Identity.
Anyone who enters the solitude of his Divine Being within,
and waiting there, becomes SMALL and HUMBLE in his own eye,
but he will glory in submission.
Then, listening, he OBEYS the "still small voice" of God
within his consciousness, [and FOLLOWS the guidance given]
and then ASCENDS into his own Divine Awareness,

and finally ATTAINS to his True Self…
[*Above the temporary "John the Baptist" beliefs*].
This means, he rises above his need to 'perfect his personality,' with the new Idea instead – that of spiritual surrendering– *surrendering to a superior Truth*, and a Superior Self Awareness…NOT to a superior power.

The Old stage of 'will power' must be SACRIFICED.. before this arrival of Illumination, and it disappears from our concerns, with the arrival of the Awareness of Light … *AS our Consciousness and Body.*

We relax into a new Identification, into our Divine Original Awareness, which takes over *operating* our **Temple Identity Life** in the spontaneity and authenticity of the now-moment. Then, our Identity, simply manifests its perfection, instead of us "trying for it." 46.

Then Jesus saw little babies being fed and said to his disciples:
These babies being NURSED are like those being nurtured into
Divine Consciousness by their Holy Breath.
For these babies work to receive their food, yet their mothers work as well.
They replied: We are humble.
Does that mean we can enter into Divine Consciousness?

Jesus said: When you, with childlike innocence and complete acceptance,
see The One in everything and everyone, as well as yourself;
and when you make the two *[your soul and body]* as equals,
also when your inner life is honored equally with your outer life;
and when you make what is without like what is within,
 — making your external activities like your spiritual guidance;
and when what is within is just like what is without,
 (as when your thoughts and words match your actions…)
and your Integrity is clear;

When you unite the male and female ASPECTS of your being,
uniting your Power and Wisdom, so that your male Soul aspect
is no longer unconscious, unbridled force
and your female Spirit aspect is no longer unconscious, compliant creativity,

CHAPTER 9 ~ *Life of Transformation*

but each, henceforth works TOGETHER, at cause and *consciously..*
by attending to, and *following* your Divine Guidance within;

This too...When you eliminate DUALISTIC "seeing" from your mind,
[*thinking that good and evil exist separately in the Universe of Divine Being*]
When you eliminate your beliefs in SEPARATION,
(**ending your beliefs in a judging, condemning Go**d)
who lives somewhere outside of you, in a distant locale called Heaven,

And replace those beliefs by seeing with the SINGLE EYE [the One "I"]
that sees One Loving Power in you, and the Universe,
in emanation and concealment – not Two powers in opposition;
and when you believe a Divine activity permeates all your affairs,
instead of believing that Your life is only *your* Life,
(in limiting your life experience with willful schemes and self-centeredness);

When you cease this endless constant defending of yourself and your ways,
but rest, instead, in a quiet state of being;
and when you enjoy true understanding, and therefore peace,
because you have given up judging life, *solely from appearances;*
and when you have let go the ego's habit of criticizing all about you
but live peaceably instead;

When you see **oneness, wholeness, and Divine Love** between you and every
thing, instead of seeing incompleteness, weakness, and separateness: and if
you nurture This Gaze and This Attitude within your Heart,
while allowing the Healing Breath to *nurture and expand your daily Vision,*
then you shall enter the Expansive Being of your Eternal Self. 22.

If your soul and flesh make peace within your conscious life and living,
and if you unify the spirit/emotion with all your *thoughts, words, and deeds,*
your unified Presence can command any life challenges to "give way" and
they WILL MOVE; for the power created by the unification of ***intention,
emotion,*** and ***love's radiant attention,*** is greater than any earthly situation
that you could encounter at any time. 48.

A man cannot ride two horses at the same time, or accurately shoot
two arrows. A servant cannot obey two different masters;
he must honor one or the other, or they will put him at cross purposes.
No one drinks in the OLD WINE of *old religious ceremonies and rituals,*
then immediately desires the NEW WINE of **inner spiritual inspiration.**
For until one leaves behind the old beliefs of separateness from God,
one does not appreciate the freedom and grace of attending
to the inner Self Awareness.

Nor can the Christ Awareness be contained in an OLD SKIN
[of the 'ego personality'] because it would break apart.
For the old identity, impure in itself, cannot withstand the power of *Divine Beingness* overshadowing it. One must increase one's vibrational frequency with breath work, exercise, meditation, and proper diet.

This raising up of one's Light Vibration allows the Christ Mind to perform its work within the body. Conversely, old awareness is not found
in a purified body-temple for the temple could perish from the poison of it, due to the debilitating nature of that old awareness.

Just as an old patch would tear if sown onto a new garment,
the old ineffective lifestyle of the former ego identity
is not suitable for the New Man Divine Persona. 47.

When you make the two into One, **uniting your breath and your flesh daily**
in new powerful ways, and when you WED your soul to your mind—
intention to thinking—you become the spiritual Offspring of humanity.
You will be called a "Son of Man" because you will be a member of a new
Divine Race on Earth — the next stage in human evolution — and
you will be a citizen of a new generation. Like a prince born from among peasants, *your Consciousness will be powerful.*
Then if you order the MOUNTAIN to move [*if you command your elevated and powerful Consciousness to serve you*], it will. 106.

Your Christed Awareness and your old self-image share each day and each night within you. They share the FOOD eaten and all aspects of your living, until the final moment.

They even share the bed on which you sleep—
but One shall Live [the *Divine Awareness* shall live]
while the other will die [the ***ego persona*** will be risen above].
On that day of Transformational Rebirth there shall be two in a bed;
One shall be taken and the other [the ego] will be left behind.

There shall be two in the FIELD [*two "identifications" in the heart*].
One shall be taken, and the other [*the ego-memories*] will be left behind.

Then Salome, thinking the Christ Awareness was only true for Jesus,
misunderstood saying "Did you at some time sleep in my bed, Master?
Or have you eaten from my table?" Jesus answered her:

"I, the Christ Light that you see, *the Divine Life in Jesus,* am actually,
the expressed Life of God, that is in all people; **'I'** am an equal in Heaven'
[***Individuality is an integral part of the Infinite Consciousness***],
and it is one-with the Infinite I AM of the Universe —
— it is an equal and individual Aspect of the Infinite One —
and is given all things that belong to the great and infinite I AM."

'I' am in equal honor, because 'I' *is the Visible expression of the I AM* —
and each of us is this expression.
This 'I' [*this Christed Awareness in each of us*]
is the One Child of the Living One in every person.
Each 'I' is the One in the Many, and the many in the One.
'I AM' is the Infinite, expressed in diversity."

Salome then responded: "I know why I am Master, I am your disciple."
Jesus replied: "But listen. When a person is growing equal to their divinity
[*raising the person's light vibration*], they are filled with their own *Divine Awareness* and is suffused with tolerance, wisdom, and love for everyone.
Also calm understanding, gracefulness, freedom, and power
will *flow from them.*

So they do not need a master, except of course the Infinite I AM,
who is awakening us to that Oneness in each of our individual lives,
and who is our very Life, heartbeat and consciousness,
and our One True Cause.

"But when a person is going away from his *Divine Interior and Natural Self,*
[toward his self-centered ego-personality]
pursuing momentary pleasures, things, and self-centeredness,
his awareness is filled with worry, frustration, and confusion.

He feels self-doubt, vacillation, and darkness,
because he regularly avoids the Love within his soul;
and this is why he regularly condemns himself and others.
All of this creates pain, violence, and sorrow.   61.

CHAPTER 9 ~ *Life of Transformation*

This *raising up* of one's Light Vibration
allows the Christ Mind to perform its work
within the body.

Splendorous Light Within

When humanity discovers this Fire Breath,
they will transform their earthly body to Light.

~ Chapter 10 ~

The Temptation: Whose Temple Is It?

Jesus In-Breathed with them and said:
"Receive you the Holy Breath."   ~John 20:22

Then he said: I AM casting a FIRE upon the world [*the Divine Breath*]
to purify, nourish, and transform the race.
When humanity discovers this Fire Breath, they will transform their earthly
body to Light. I rekindle this awareness until it BURNS us into Light
beings everywhere [until Divine Breath purifies everyone]
and all of us, as a single Divine Child, ascend into the **One I AM**. 10.

He who is close to Me is close to the Fire of Divine Inspiration,
for it transforms the propensities of the physical form and the ego-brain.
He who is far from Me is distant from that healing, transforming Breath
and that enlightening Spiritual Awareness. 82.

ADAM, (the human phase in the evolving Divine Self Awareness)
arrived here with great power and abundance; taking authority
over the earth scene, utilizing great ingenuity in subduing it.
Even so, he, as an evolutionary step, is not adequate to express
your capability, your power, or your Divine Heritage.

As a stepping stone, the ADAM identification
is not deserving of your continued attention; as Is the Christ Mind,
who is your new interior master and your next stage.

The distinction of a master is his loving life force and his power.
Had the ADAM PHASE been truly advanced with breath and body
united as a Conscious Force, he would not have "*tasted death*".
But the divided human awareness identifies with the body as 'identity',
seeing itself as separate from Divine Life and separate from the Breath.

Ego believes the Spirit Breath is something that passes in and out
of the body, instead of seeing it somehow being 'One and the Same'
as our Human Life.
Your Divine Awareness, however, is of Wholeness —
— of Heaven and Earth, within and without, spirit and flesh as One.
It is a Oneness ... and it transforms livingness into lovingness. 85.

Then Jesus — the Christ-**Man** – the embodiment of pure individual being,
asked his disciples, "Compare me to someone. Tell me whom I resemble?"
Peter replied: "You're like a righteous angel."
Matthew continued: "Or like a wise philosopher."
But Thomas said:
"Truthfully, Master, I cannot bring myself to utter comparisons to you."

Jesus came to Thomas and quietly said:
"I am no longer your master.
You have drunk from the bubbling Fountain of Life which I brought,
and now you are drunk with the discovery of your Spiritual Breath
and of Divine Being within your heart,
which from now on will lead you and from now on you will obey."

Then Jesus took Thomas aside and gave him three words.
[Probably a mantra, such as "I AM I" – the Divine Name,
to reinforce and strengthen Thomas's newly formed consciousness of self].

The other disciples came to Thomas asking: "What did Jesus say to you?"
Thomas replied:
"If I told you the words he gave to me,
you'd probably be shocked or you would become belligerent or
argumentative, and would hurl STONES [spiritual truths and principles]
At me ... accusing me of blasphemy, whereupon FIRE
[the purifying divine spirit-breath teaching that Jesus gave them]
would rise truly from the STONES [from your arguments about Truth]
and your arguments about Truth, would inevitably point to this Truth
Jesus gives, and your words would BURN and Indict you instead." 13.

Then some of those disciples said to Jesus:
"Tell us who you really are, so that we may believe in you."
He replied: "You are testing the FACE of Heaven and Earth.
You are studying *The All* [the manifest universe]
without recognizing the Divine One that inhabits everything and everyone.
You do not see God, literally everywhere. But you do not even know how
to truly live in just this moment, ***without*** an agenda.

"When you finally see *'The I'* within yourself, you will emotionally melt in
joy and you will know that the *I AM and the 'I'*—Its manifest expression—
are One. If you have seen *'the I' within,* you have seen your I AM Self. 91.

When you perceive one not born of woman
[seeing the Christ Expression perform its work within you]
then lay Down your ego personality and its mental habit patterns,
with which you have identified and protected all these years,
and just let them go. STOP leaning on your old habits.
Live spontaneously now, in the moment, without an agenda, and you
will be led by the Divine One, and you will live in the frequency of Bliss.

Humbly honor only that birth-less and death-less Divine Life Force in you.
Worship That One ... with time spent together .. within.
Make the purification and vibrational increase of your Temple [body]
the first priority; for that is the first glimmering of re-union
with the great I AM of you, in you, as you. 15.

"I the **Divine One,** am the Light. "I" am the true Self Awareness
and Expressed Image everywhere; and it is "I" that shines throughout
the manifest universe, especially in humanity. I AM I.
The ALL came from Me .. the One Self and incorporeal Life.
I AM divine cause, creativity, and expression in *unified* operation.
I AM living everywhere in everything. Now The ALL [*the external expression*]
is returning to ME, becoming Aware of Me.
SPLIT WOOD [*look between each of your thoughts and your teachings*]
and I AM there, within.
RAISE a STONE [esteem truth] and you will find Me everywhere." 77.

Come to Me ... for my yoke is Light [my admonition is Self awareness].
My leading is gentle ... and in Me you shall find rest and comfort. 90.

Then they said: "*Master, you must Be the* ... You are the one all 24 prophets
of Israel spoke of ... They have prophesied of *you* all these centuries."
Jesus replied: "*You are still neglecting The One, who lives in your Presence
in order to talk about the dead.*" 52.

The disciples said to him: "Why do you say that to us?"
Jesus replied: "You do not understand the I AM from what I say.
You've become like the Jewish philosophers who love only the words,
the study and discussions – [the philosophic system — *the TREE*] –
but they hate the growth and the transformational nature
of spiritual living [the fruit]."
"You love the FRUIT of the Kingdom [*the benefits of Divine Awareness*]
but hate the path of within-ness, and its discipline of focusing on God
to dismantle ego patterns, [*those habits and identifications you have ingrained
in your consciousnes*s] and which you still think of, as your identity." 43.

Here is a parable to illustrate: A virtuous LANDLORD [Divine Being]
owned a VINEYARD [*the visible universe and the human Heart/Temple*]
which he leased to TENANT FARMERS [*to the children of this earth-life*]
so they could TILL it and develop FRUITS from the LAND
[*develop an Awareness of spiritual oneness in their Heart and Mind*].
Then the Landlord would receive FRUIT from them as PAYMENT
[*receive an evolved and spiritual awareness from his Individual Expressions, –
His-Her children*].

Then Divine Being sent a SERVANT [holy man, guru, or prophet]
to remind them to make PAYMENT [to develop spiritually];
but he was seized, beaten, and almost killed.

When the servant returned to tell his master of this,
the Landlord thought, perhaps they had not recognized the servant
so he sent another, but they beat up him, too.

Then the Landlord sent his Son, thinking they would respect his SON
[*that growing Divine Awareness within their hearts*].
However, their egos knew that '*indulging an ILLUMINATION*'
[*from the Begotten SON-ship*] would be the end of the human ego.
So they KILLED him [*ignoring their own inner divine awareness, pointed out by the Begotten One*]. So, friends LET GO of your **addictive ego-habit-persona,** while you are in this world, and RISE into letting your Christ Self express, while you are still within "Time." 65.

Blessed are you if you know the TIME of the ROBBER'S ARRIVAL —
— knowing when and where TEMPTATION comes in your life —
and, where, in your life, the BATTLE for dominion most likely will occur.
Which... shall rule over your consciousness, the world's attractions
or the Divine Life within you?

When temptation comes, turn within and ask your spiritual Beingness
to lift you out of it and *change your desires.*
Breathe deeply to calm your nature. Turn away from the temptation.
Do not continue to *look upon* the unclean thing *even pondering its qualities.*
Do not lean upon your own will power to overcome it;
at best, it's temporary, and this is because it is still
of the ego's mental structure,
and it does not draw you closer to your Divine Soul Awareness
but reinforces your beliefs of a *separate* strength and supposed *aloneness.*

Doing these things, you can prepare yourself and rise in meditation,
and collect yourself in prayer, and unite yourself in the deep, rhythmic
Conscious Breath, unifying soul and body as One Power.
Then you can stand prepared against the ego's temptations. 103.

Remember, nothing can enter your Temple Consciousness or upset your
life's progress if you are unifying your inner spiritual awareness with
your external activities. Nor can your life be seized by any force.
The Father of Lights has given dominion to each of us over our own being.
There is no need to worry over dark forces or spirits threatening your life;
it is, in fact, they who will shy away from your Light.

Do not fear anything invisible.
However, if your *inner spiritual activities* [your RIGHT HAND]
and *your outer earthly activitie*s [your LEFT HAND] are at cross purposes
and in conflict, then your current progress [your mental HOUSE]
can be ransacked.
Remember, if our Heart is divided against itself
it cannot stand unified, in strength.

Live your true and highest Awareness, and you will be a fortress of Strength
Do not live in contradictions, but abide yourself in pure
singleness of Purpose. Do not try living "spiritually" for only one day,
and live the other days otherwise.

Do not go against your "conscience" [*a pure messenger of God*].
Raise your vibratory level every day. Go within yourself to Feel
your Higher Self's wisdom-choices ... and Rest in those. 35.

He that has the understanding of *Oneness With* shall continually receive
or *experience* that which he is One With.. through the Law of Attraction,
whether it be spiritual or physical.
But to him that has not this truth of Oneness-With, even the things
he currently possesses he shall LOSE, through the
Law of Disassociation, and the Principle of Repulsion. 41.

If we repudiate or deny the existence **of our I AM Self** (*our Soul and Father-cause — **disassociating our human persona from our divine Beingness***)
this Can be rectified.. and we can experience an interior forgiveness
in heart and mind; because.. our Original Cause and True Being
are unaffected by our human ig*Norance*.

Now, if we hate or ignore 'the body' of our *current spiritual state* [the SON]
and if we belittle our current expression [*bemoaning our life situation*]
or complain over our *current unfoldment* and abilities,
We Can correct this too; for our hatred is pointed only toward today ...
And today's current condition can always be risen above and improved.

Nor will we be trapped in our old personality, or the condemnation it felt.
However if we ignore the maternal Holy Breath of Divine essence and Mind
(our creative intelligence and purifying power)
We're ignoring our Inspiration, Intuition, and Conscience,
And we are breaking our own personal trust.

When we do not practice breathing the Sacred Breath, for its purification process, we are ignoring the powers of growth, transformation, and healing *in our life,* and we're pushing away the nurturing
Divine Hand in daily moments.

All this Love *is given freely to us so that we may rise up* into our true self in unhindered Grace, **while on Earth,** to rise above the physical tomb of ego.

The Holy Breath-spirit is our facility that expands our human awareness and transforms our body to light.

Our breath allows ascension out of the down-pulling
ego tendencies that enslave humanity.

We might as well banish ourselves to the "far country" of sorrow
for turning away the maternal "*helping hand of breathing the Breath-Spirit*"
and its loving guidance.

Whenever the igNorance of our Holy Breath occurs,
and its powers of purification and its inner inspiration are absent
from the mental and physical activities of our life,
they are also missing from our **Conscious Spiritual Awareness**.

How then can this *ig-Norance and Refusal* of Divine Guidance
be *'for..Given'*
in either the material realm of the body, or in the etheric realm of ur consciousness, when…
[it is not even received] … or practiced?   44.

Splendorous Light Within

The journey requires a dedication to interiority
and a *single-minded attention* to achieving
the pure and permanent Identity.

THE SOLITARY ONE:
In the Light

"Be still ... know ... I AM God."
~Psalms 46:10

Blessed are the ONES who have unified their Intention, Attention,
and Expression with divine solitude — [the SOLITARY];
and blessed are "the Elect,"
[those consciously dedicated to their divine reunification]
for they shall live in bliss, in their true Home, in eternity and light,
and they shall find rest in their Original Soul awareness. 49.

They said: "Lord, there is so much mental advice regarding
our subconscious mind.
And this religious input sounds holy and seems spiritual, but there's no real
help from it, for removing the ache within our heart, nor for truly assisting
us to ascend out of our mental discontent, which we constantly endure
[*in the emptiness that our ego-mind continually experiences*]." 74

He replied: "Yes, there is help... *transformation deserves assistance,*
but truly anointed *Christed* Teachers are scarce.
So in prayer see, and joyfully feel, the I AM sending your Light Self
into your ripened heart...to rebirth and breathe you,
 — another Divine Child — who is ready for The Change." 73.

A woman from the crowd said to him:
Blessed is the womb that gave you birth and the woman that nursed you."
He replied: "Blessed are those who have heard the Word of the I AM
and heeded that pure Christ Awareness within,
and who have obeyed The Word, maintaining themselves in Truth
through maintaining attunement with their Deep Self.

This Word 'I AM' is always near you.. in your mouth and in your heart,
so that you readily may find it and experience its
transformational, guiding power.
A day will come when many will say:
'Blessed are the barren or childless ones,
who used the time that would have been spent raising children
to enter their Expansive Light Being within
and have given birth to their Spiritual Persona instead.' 79.

Any one who does not turn toward the inner I AM – surrendering the
earthly father and mother, and brothers and sisters of this world,
 — not giving up their old ways, taking up their "cross," as I did,
 — not putting away their former life, giving up their old routines
 — but seeking their Original Life Force instead—cannot become worthy
of ME — their Whole Self. For it takes reorganizing, one's life-priorities.

The journey requires a dedication to interiority
and a *single-minded attention* to achieving the pure and permanent Identity.
Remember, one who travels alone, travels far.

So if we let our family pressure us, or lead us away from the inner pursuit
of our solitude experiences,
we cannot enter into our wondrous and powerful Self Awareness. 55.

In nature, foxes have lairs, birds have nests, and everything in the world
has its own place. However, the spiritually born offspring of humanity—
the "Sons of Mankind" – those newly transformed Children of Light
and new members of Earth's Divine Race – have no 'worldly' thing
in which to Rest their mind, [*providing spiritual nourishment*]
as *focusing on* our Divine *Consciousness* does.
For their contemplative home, is in the "I AM Light"
and they are merely transients of this beautiful world
and its dualistic hypnotic system.   86.

Mary Magdalen said to Jesus: "*Tell us what your disciples are like and how they should be in the world when you are gone.*"
Jesus replied: "Their life is like a FARMER [one with a spiritual path] who discovers STRANGERS [temptations] traveling through, and they camp in the FIELD 'of his heart.. where they do not belong'. And when the *Farmer of the FIELD* [disciple] discovers these temptations, he orders them *Out of his heart-space,* so the intruders quietly depart, leaving his mind and heart-space unburdened."

So be as wise in this world as those who are users of the system.
If someone knows to expect trouble before it happens,
like expecting a THIEF at a certain place and time,
[*like a temptation which regularly arises in one's life*]
then be prepared against the dangerous entry,
block the way and protect your consciousness from *painful mistakes.*

Be wary of the world system, with its dominating influences
and its down-pulling temptations, persons, and attractions.
It will make you its brother and its honored guest.
And then like a THIEF in the night, it will rob you blind
in your unsuspecting darkness. Therefore, prepare yourself daily.

Seek your divine Awareness Early, in your day and in your life that you may always feel the Presence within, while you work and while you play. When you go in and go out in all your activities, maintain this watchfulness on the Inner Presence, and it will lead you and live through you as you, and you shall feel insight and power that is humbling.

Ever before you sleep, graciously and with gratitude Surrender the operation of your consciousness [temple-path] to your all-knowing Self, *that Original Soul Spirit Expression whose divine right is to live this life,* that you thought belonged to your ego-habits and daily patterns.

It is up to you to surrender the past of the ego personality.
It is up to you to willingly release your consciousness back to your I AM, before you sleep at night, with consent and harmony.
Let it be like keeping an appointment with a lover, that is honored tenderly.

Go to rest at night with loving gratitude, and rise up each day
in partnership with Divine Being.
Practice this Presence ceaselessly throughout the day, and have patience
toward yourself and your efforts.

Let no self-condemning judgment rise up in you, but stay in balance,
even with life's vicissitudes.
This being done, you shall be lifted up and exalted with the Highest,
and you shall live life in grace, with abundance and peace.

No THIEVES [no ego impulses] shall enter your being to steal
your confidence or destroy your tranquility ... for you will be in the Power.

So be as zealous in your pursuits, as the children of darkness are in theirs;
for the benefits you expect and the fruits you anticipate from walking the
spiritual path will be found. *So... "How do you live in this world ..?
And what does the Lord Require of you?" It's Simple.
Do justly, Love Mercy, and at all times Humbly Walk with Your God
within — by attending to the graceful feelings of bliss within you.*

May there arise within you a WISE ONE [*your portion of your Holy Breath*]
which will manifest in this world, as our True Self, when It is ready
and while we are still within "Time".
Let him who understands, act, asking his inner Lord to transform him
when his 'time' is ripe. 21.

After this has transpired, if people ask about the origin
of your powerful Awareness, answer:
"*We arose out of the Light of Infinite Awareness, where projected visible
light came out of itself—out of its Resting State — from its invisible
formless Being; and it "rested from work" in us, as it formed our
"moving image," and our holographic Self Awareness.*

If you are asked regarding your spiritual Identity, answer this way:
"*We are Children of the Living Light, and we are the Expressed Image
emerging from the Living Light of Divine Being."*

If ever you are asked what is the sign of Divine Being, answer:
"*Movement and Rest, the In-breath and Out-breath, our Heart Beating,
— emanation and concealment — the One and the many,
and invisible Life and visible Expression.*" 50.

His disciples asked him, When will this Divine Kingdom come
and cover the whole earth and everyone therein. Jesus said:
"God's Kingdom [Consciousness] will never come as an observable event
the way you are expecting it.
No one will ever say, '*Look, there! It is arriving,*'
or 'Look over here in this mountain. It has finally come.' [Q]

Because the Kingdom of God is not a visible appearing.
It is within you ... invisible to human eyes.
"It is the spiritual guidance of Divine Being within, that transforms our
heart and our actions. It arrives in each of us in our own time. Gradually
this Kingdom increases on the earth plane, as each one of us manifests its
Presence, day by day, first one, then another, then the whole; but it is You
who points yourself toward its entrance, and it is You who walks in.

The invisible governing Power of I AM and its omnipresent
spiritual Consciousness is already spread throughout Heaven and Earth,
sustaining everything, yet no man sees it.
It is seen in the masterpiece of the Universe, *its visible expression.*
It does not even need to arrive, for this Kingdom is here right now.

So unless you pursue your spirituality and are dedicated to arriving in the
consciousness of bliss and power, in your inner I AM,
this Divine Heart and Consciousness will remain invisible to you.
You must *feel* this Awareness.

To feel it you must go back into the Deep of your Consciousness.
You must be born from Above in the renewal of spontaneity in your life,
seeing without predisposed expectations or negative thought-taking,
just letting go the past.
This way you will perceive freshly the purity of each now-moment,

and you shall cleanse your moment-to-moment fluid Awareness
of all worldly identifications by continually focusing inward
on that pure awareness;
and you shall daily **raise the quality** of your Sea of Consciousness
through contemplative meditation, experiential visualization,
and consistent heart-felt prayer — dedicated to you and Everyone.

For what you can give to another, you yourself can also receive.
Doing these things will transform the thought projections
of your human heart, where they originate and live.
You will feel and think from a higher vibration.

And once accomplished, you will rise higher in the Consciousness of bliss.
Also, you must be "born" a 2nd time in the Divine Breath — born in the
realization *that your Conscious Breath* is God's Movement and Rest in you.
In the spiritual life, it is known as.. the "purifying fire."
When you know that this Breath is your bodily connection to the *infinite Living One*, and along with consciousness, is your portion of Divine Being,
then you shall experience the "fire of transformation"
and find that Kingdom in your Center, as your life force.

Thereafter, you will always feel the Divine One moving powerfully
as your life. So if you start the journey back, away from your ego nature,
and with a "wave of determination" will dedicate yourself in earnest
to this progress, you shall be met by your Divine Self Awareness,
while you are yet a "long way off,"
and there shall be celebration over your Divine Re-union. [R]. 113.

You see, the Divine envelops us.
Images of light appear all around us, in every moment of life.
We see these lighted "forms" as 'everything' in our environment.
And there is within these lighted images, a ***Living Mind - Presence,***
which is hidden behind the reflected light in
the outer "form" of everything;
however… it Lives and Breathes within "The Travelers" —
– the "visible" Children of God.
This Divine I AM reveals *itself and its Essence* personally to each of us. 83.

In that day, Divine Being shall be unveiled to you as your inner I AM,
-as your transpersonal heart-level Awareness
and your life will never be the same.

Your inner Image, *of this holographic Light Body,* will be revealed to your
Awareness, and will be Unfurled before your vision…
and you shall know it, as your "body's" *Traveling form.*

Your Identity as a Living One — a traveling Light Child and visible "I" —
will be known by you
To be an Individual Image of the Living ONE — the Omnipresent I —
who is our Resting Infinite Light Being, and our invisible I AM.

You are the Image and Likeness of Divine Being…

And you are infinitely loved .. and you are assured in this truth.
If you know this, you will neither see "death", nor know fear ever again.

Realize, this world ***cannot restrain the ones*** who find their Deep I AM. 111

THE END

the Amplified Interpreted
~ Gospel According to Thomas ~

Author's Note

I have personally found that re-reading spiritual material frequently, over considerable time, has granted a significantly deeper comprehension within, and a transformation of awareness can therefore occur for us. Practicing the Holy Breath unifies us, in a Oneness with our Divine Life Force-Source. Through growing "a movement and a rest" awareness in each moment, at last we Breathe a release of ego. It comes with endless sighs of grace, and then… Gratitude overwhelms our heart, and expands our Mind and our very Being. This is the gift of The Divine Breath in us… which Jesus Christ gave to our awareness.

PAGE/VERSE LOCATOR

Chapter	'Title Page'	Pg.	Verse #
(chapter 1)	The Decision To Journey Back to the Light	100	1, 2, 67, 17
		102	23, 62, 94, 92
		103	27, 88
		104	78
		105	39, 102
		112	30
(chapter 2)	Leaving the World Behind	115	28, 56
		117	16, 72,105
		118	112, 80
		121	60, 42
(chapter 3)	The Growth of the Inner Child	123	38, 8
		124	12
		125	37, 99, 101
		126	114, 108
		127	100
(chapter 4)	The Path of Grace: Friendship With the Divine	133	36, 70
(chapter 5)	The Path of Ascension: Uniting Spirituality With the Inner Life	135	6
		138	14, 45
		139	6, 7, 59
		140	104, 53, 87
		141	19, 89, 26
		142	34, 31, 93, 25
(chapter 6)	Living Amid the Challenges and Tests	145	54, 58, 68
		146	69
		147	3
		148	66
		151	18
(chapter 7)	Reunification: Your Discipline and Destination	152	4, 29, 32
		153	33, 5
		154	84
		155	75

THE QUOTATIONS IN *'THOMAS'*

[A] John 14:19
[B] John 14:23
[C] Acts 17:28
[D] II Cor. 6:16
[E] Matt. 6:26-30
[F] Prov. 3:6
[G] Matt. 6:5
[H] Matt. 6:4, 6
[I] Ascribed to an ancient Indian Master

Chapter	'Title Page'	Pg.	Verse #
(chapter 8)	The Kingdom of Heaven: Our Ever-Expansive Expanding Awareness	159	20, 40
		160	9
		161	57
		162	107, 96
		163	97, 76
		164	98, 109
		165	64, 63
		166	81, 95, 110, 51
(chapter 9)	Living Daily the Life of Transformation	169	71, 24
		171	11
		172	46
		173	22, 48
		174	47, 106
		176	61
(chapter 10)	The Temptation: Whose Temple Is It?	179	10, 82
		180	85, 13
		181	91, 15, 77
		182	90, 52, 43
		183	65, 103
		184	35. 41
		185	44
(chapter 11)	The Solitary One: In the Light	187	49, 74, 73
		188	79, 55, 86
		190	21
		191	50
		192	113, 83
		193	111

[J] John 3:23
[K] II Cor. 6:4
[L] Matt. 4:17
[M] Luke 17:21
[N] Psalm 139:2-10
[O] John 14:6

[P] John 14:10
[Q] Matt. 24:26
[R] Luke 15:20
[S] Mic. 6:8
[T] Dan. 5:23

[U] Eph. 4:4-6
[V] Isa. 26:3
[W] Isa. 30:15
[X] Kahlil Gibran
"The Prophet"

We can never say "I love You" enough
to Divine Being, for providing The All,
and all the experiences and enjoyment thereof,
through eternity.

SACRED POWER
For Purification and Elevation

Let's share an extraordinarily powerful *Holy Breath* exercise. To put it simply, this is for transformational endeavors. Performing this exercise over months or years will transform one's sense of Self, and one's power-base within awareness, toward a Light that is one's Divine nature. And remember, this is meant to be practiced daily our entire life. We do not stop doing this one day as if we have arrived, or finally accomplished something; as if we got all we could from it. The reason? The reason is two-fold. First is we can never Grow in awareness enough. We will always and Ever have more continuing awareness and more enlightenment to accumulate and appreciate.

Secondly, we can never say "I love You" enough to Divine Being, for providing The All, and all the experiences and enjoyment thereof, through eternity. If someone fed you a masterpiece of dining enjoyment every single day would you ever stop saying Thank you? …of course not. These breathing exercises are a way of *embracing and expressing gratitude* to our Father-Mother God. Practicing these exercises also makes US more powerful, capable individuals in whatever realm we may find our self. These exercises also create another truly advanced outlet through which God can perform greater works of love and power in this three dimensional universe; in us. It's in fact increasing the number of Christ-like individuals in the environment to do these exercises. The power that one feels, and is changed by — that one IS, humbles us. But there is an ancillary *power and Gift* in performing this loving discipline. Yes, breathing the Breath of God does its awesome work in us, but **the time spent in it** is *a sign* to Divine Being of *your personal Love* God-ward.

Just scheduling the time and endeavor transforms you and your life and God *rewards it*. Performing this breath work effects a change of one's personal understanding toward one's identity. Eventually, one begins seeing one's self more as Light than matter — more as Love than Pain — more as Joy than sorrow. While you do this exercise you may include visualization and/or prayer during its endeavor. In fact, it is advised that you Do this combining of spiritual technologies at simultaneous moments within your practice. This way you empower the whole exercise with an elevated and sacred purpose.

This exercise includes a brief holding and an expelling of the breath for specific durations of time. Let us discuss some ancient words regarding aspects of our marvelous bodily being. *Ida* (eeda) and *Pingala* (Ping-gulah) are ancient Sanskrit words for the Sympathetic nerve-channel / Left side, and the Para-sympathetic nerve channel /Right side of our Spinal column. This Pathway of spinal nerve fibers carries Life Force energy up and down the body each moment. What's amazing is the nerve fiber network covers essentially every three dimensional centimeter of our bodies, making us connected to and sensorily stimulated by the outside world in amazing ways.

I'm constantly in awe that the most insignificant nerve stimulations such as a tiny puff of air is felt distinctly on my bodily form, whether my knee, neck, arm, ankle—it doesn't matter where. Temperature differences are *instantly* felt by us. The tiniest feelings are known. The body is a miracle of 'sensing.' And all these nerve fibers covering our entire physical being are fed by the sympathetic and parasympathetic nerve channels in our spinal column. The life-force electrical energy that travels through our nerve network is Divine and universal power, downloaded into our body, giving us an experience of the three-dimensional universe. Your electrical neuronic energy is one and the same, as the cosmic energy that fills every space, in our entire cosmos. The energy out there is the same energy in here. It is the same Divine Power everywhere, in God's omnipresence, and it's in you.

The left and right nostrils are connected to these nerve pathways. In spiritual disciplines, we are to take command of our bodily and spiritual energies on their Pathway within our body and Being; and that is why we are practicing these exercises. Masters use this 'energy command' for purposes of healing, touching higher realms, and experiencing Higher States of Consciousness. When we breathe from side to side in the manner being described to you here, we are balancing the positive and negative forces within us in the morning and evening (that are caused by the agitated daily forces around us).

When doing this exercise in the Morning one begins breathing through the Left Nostril and In the Evening, one begins the exercise breathing through the Right Nostril. This means we hold down the other nostril while breathing in. This breath exercise should be done, as close to sunrise and sundown as possible…but where it's not possible, do not worry over it. It is better to DO this exercise than not to do it. One may also do this exercise at anytime that one wishes. As much time and energy as one dedicates to this endeavor, is as much as one can feel transformational progress.

There is something about the 'control' of the intake and release of the breath that creates our ability to participate in this energy, and sometimes it causes an awesome, powerful 'state of expansion', inner heat, and an indescribable loving sense of expanding Radiant Energy (which sometimes feels like it may "burst" us). One senses and therefore learns about an expanded "State of Beingness" in this kind of exercise; and one may relate to one's self as an infinite Life Force; (*this is perhaps why one feels like one may burst*). Of course it never does burst us, but it feels like it may… however, the immense unexplainable expansiveness of this Power is such that, all we can say after experiencing it, is one is in a state of absolute and thorough humility and awe at the love felt (one may drop one's head in complete deference). One just 'beholds' the experience. One simply feels without thought or evaluation, except for Awe. And one may almost lose consciousness during the exercise *(one often could if one did not have a full intention to maintain consciousness)*. But please remain conscious at all times; do not Lose conscious awareness *(don't faint or fall asleep)*. It is the *conscious experience* of this power and inspiration that is meaningful. *In–Spire* literally means to *in-breathe* (and it means '*from God*') and this is what you are doing. So, if during the indraw or Hold of Breath you feel your awareness drifting away to unconsciousness then hold off on the remainder of it a moment, to bring your full awareness back up, then continue.

I will say right now this exercise *Is* a **most powerful** one. Let it be said though, that if one goes into this exercise *just 'for the experiences'* one is tainting one's motive, and The Power recedes away from curious entertainment value. We must be in here for its expanding, lifting, cleansing benefits not its extraordinary or interesting qualities. If one is seeking The One for entertainment, *The One* knows the motivation and will allow one to prove one's self with perseverance and honest seeking, as one is willing to simply receive whatever Divine Being will give to one without an attempt at controlling-demanding it. So, when it happens it happens. We are doing this to be cleansed, not to be entertained. Do it for the cleansing inspirational purpose. Note: when we hold our breath in the exercises here Visualize only Good things Prayerfully. Pausing your Breath is a very powerful moment indeed.

At SUNRISE And SUNSET

Now when performing this exercise you Sit with a Straight Back... placing the Spine in an erect position. As we have said, in the morning one begins by breathing IN through the Left Nostril by depressing down the Right Nostril; but, one does this Left Nostril complete Inhale spanning Four Heartbeats...

For example: (*One thousand 1, One thousand 2, One thousand 3, One thousand 4*);
THEN one Holds this breath IN for SIXTEEN Heartbeats
(*One thousand 1, One thousand 2, One thousand 3, etc.*).
THEN one expels this HELD BREATH over Eight Heartbeats
(*One thousand 1, One thousand 2...etc.*)

BUT...one does this expelling through the RIGHT NOSTRIL (during the morning exercise).

Then one draws the next Breath in on the same Four Heartbeat count but this time it is drawn through the Right Nostril
(by holding down the Left Nostril)... **and the inhale is immediate with no pause between.**

Remember this...there is no pause between exhales and inhales... always, it is immediate.

Then once again *it is held down there for 16 Heartbeats* and it is released through the opposite (or Left) nostril over an Eight Heartbeat count.

Now here's one very important point. The Eight Beat exhale you may find challenging to accomplish. (*You may find your pushing out the air faster than eight heart beats, but it does not mean you should stop before the eight beats expire*). You should modulate your exhale so it's measured. You'll have to use your diaphragm to push out *till the expiration of the Eight count.* You may even be surprised that you are still pushing out Air!

This Left/Right complete breath pattern is done a total of Eight times in both the morning and evening exercise. This number corresponds to the seven basic Energy centers in the body, and the single Energy center just above the body—over the crown of the head—which connects us to Infinite Divine Being. Called *chakras* in eastern writing, it is a center of bodily nerve energy (*rotating/spinning moving energy*) built into our Being, and, they are located at seven ascending centers associated with our nerve junctions, connecting to our vital parts and inner glandular systems-array.

So on each of these *eight sets of breaths,* we are bringing the breath down to one chakra center respectively, lowest first, 1st, 2nd, 3rd, etc.; *one on each breath* – and one then harmonizes the energies there during that sixteen beat count. There is an ascending Frequency Vibration to each Chakra in the body and a certain Color associated with it.

The first one is at the base of the spine where all those nerve fibers terminate, before spreading out, and it's called the root chakra. This is also where the 'Liquid Light' *divine fire energy* resides within each of us, and is raised from. This rising energy has an ancient name from in ancient languages called kundalini energy. It is an ancient spiritual essence 'of Light' planted within us by Divine Being (mostly unknown to society, particularly modern society). It provides an *evolutionary impulse and directive in the individual and the collective.* It is a liquid light, spark of God in each of us. It's this fact that causes some spiritually oriented individuals, like masters, teachers, healers, and Messiahs such as Christ, to be far more advanced, powerful and empowering/uplifting individuals than the unevolved common person. The kundalini energy provides a higher level guidance in soul-advancement, for you the individual (*you are not doing this transformation by yourself with your small fund of knowledge*). It awakens and provides extraordinary spiritual experiences in us as it does its daily work. Practicing the Sacred Breath awakens and stirs this kundalini Light Energy to rise within your physio/psychic/spiritual being.

It will awaken each of us eventually but it can also be encouraged by us to do its work, through our intentions and spiritual disciplines. It's at the bottom end of the spine coiled like a *"liquid pearl of Light"* and its journey is up the spine, and it awakens/rectifies each chakra's energies as it travels upward. As it does so, it awakens the spiritual nature of the individual and can create a halo of personal energy. We are to consciously participate in raising this Liquid Light energy from the base of our spine up through our body, through each 'chakra center', and release our Individual Energy INTO the Cosmic Energy of *The One,* and mingle ourselves with The One and The ALL of everyone else. By doing so, we complete our selves. We take on the Infinite Wisdom of The One

Splendorous Light Within

SAMPLE BREATH TECHNIQUE IN THE A.M.

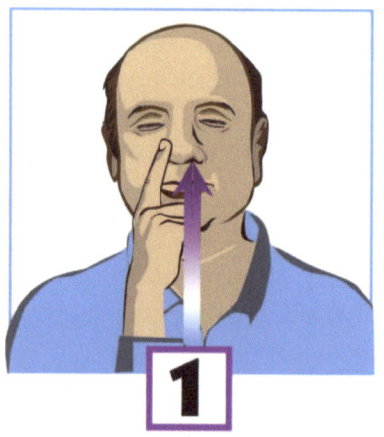

Cover right nostril with right forefinger, then INhale a blast of air through the left, count silently to 4: ("one-thousand-one, one-thousand-two, one-thousand-three, one-thousand-four")

HOLD air in lungs, counting to 16: ("one-thousand-one, one-thousand-two...etc., to sixteen)

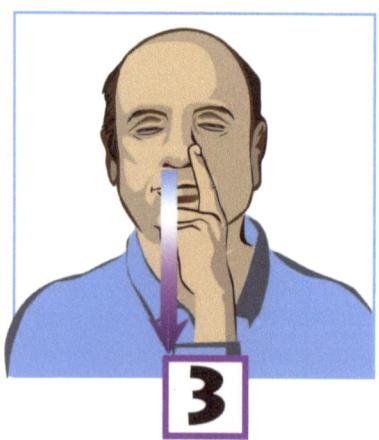

Cover Left nostril with Left forefinger, now, EXhale thru right nostril, counting to 8: ("one-thousand-one, one-thousand-two...etc.) till empty. Lift finger.

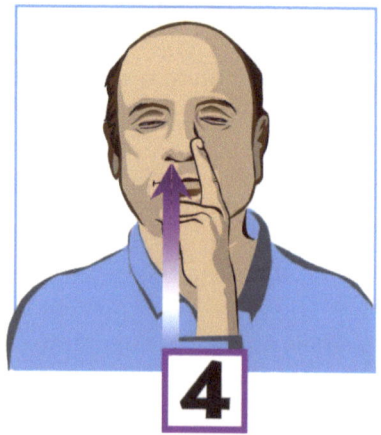

Cover left nostril with left forefinger, and INhale 4 counts thru Right, then HOLD 16 counts, then EXhale 8 counts, as before but now through the left nostril.

and the experiential knowledge of our brothers and sisters, who reside within The All as we do. We are freed of the minute parameters and belief systems of the tiny ego-Me, and rejoin the oneness, as an Integral member of The All. We are inseparable from and necessary to everyone else including *The One* — who is expressing *Us* just as He-She is expressing everyone of us, Jesus, Buddha, Krishna or anyone else you may name.

Also realize one thing. With each Exhale, you should know, that Poisons are leaving your body. One primary way that toxins leave our cells in our body is through exhalation. This is medical science, not theory. So realize and appreciate that benefit…in each Exhale…you are purifying yourself. The colors associated in each chakra are *red, orange, yellow, green, blue, mauve and white,* in that order upward. These are the colors corresponding to the bodily chakras, and you may see Etheric White or pure essence of light for the eighth chakra, which exists above the head. All these centers are to be empowered by this liquid Light, rectified, balanced and raised up by it.

	8th Chakra (etheric)	over the top of the head—is our entry, connecting space to God's mind.
	7th Chakra (white)	is inside near the top of the Head — the Pineal-connect-Point to Divinity.
	6th Chakra (mauve)	is behind the eye-brows and relates to the Personal Divine (Christ) mind and your Individuality. It relates to the Pituitary gland, and what is called the '3rd eye.'
	5th Chakra (blue)	is located in the throat and relates to The Word and Communication.
	4th Chakra (green)	is at the Heart and relates to Love.
	3rd Chakra (yellow)	is located at the solar plexus and relates to Personal power.
	2nd Chakra (orange)	is the sexual or Creative Power chakra.
	Root Chakra (red)	is located at the base of the spine near to where the coiled Liquid Light Is.

SO, when one breathes in these breaths and Holds them for 16 beats… one is Seeing and Focusing on the Color and Function associated with each level…particularly when breathing At each numbered breath pattern. For example, when one is on the fourth level of this breathing exercise (at the Heart) one sees and focuses on the color Green; and when one is at the 6th level, one focuses on Mauve.. and the function of that particular center, and so on.

However, it is strongly recommended that when one is in the process of counting the sixteen heartbeats at each and every level of this Left/Right breathing process, that one 'sees' a Lifting of one's Kundalini energy Up To and Through the color of the center one is AT, *at that moment,* and then with each of the other levels in the body that one goes through (*as one proceeds upward*). Then, when one reaches the top (eighth) chakra leading to the Universal Life force, one unites one's energy with The Universal Divine Energy. This way you unite and strengthen your kundalini energy with each of the color/qualities and essential strengths of the respective Chakra centers you move through, as your Kundalini energy moves UP and your chakras also are purified and rectified by the kundalini light.

So one should count 16 heartbeats at each Chakra level, in the "16 heartbeat count" *when one arrives there* (during this 'kundalini lifting' exercise). As one exhales the breath after the 16 count, you 'see' the kundalini rising up and out the crown of the head. This mingles your Kundalini energy with the Universal. So, there are sixteen counts at each of your eight energetic centers. Also remember because there are eight levels, and on the left and right nostrils *both,* it is therefore a sixteen aspected exercise, because you do each level TWICE, for the left and right side.

Of course, in the evening all of this is reversed — starting at the Right Nostril, instead of the left; and as each complete Right/Left pattern is done, one would do it on each of the eight chakra levels in the evening too. This whole exercise takes about 8 minutes, but when you add the warm-up exercises of deep breathing for a few minutes, which are definitely advised…along with prayer, it can become about 18 or 20 minutes at a sitting. This is just one repetition of the exercise; you may do it again and again if you like…and when you add a visualization or Prayer to it with all of the desires or goals you have, and the personal qualities that you wish to manifest in your life, it becomes even more powerful. In fact if one misses out on prayer during this exercise one has missed an enormous and powerful opportunity. But remember, silence is bless'ed too. Soon enough one will learn the 'time-frame' for counting these 'heartbeats' in each of the three phases, and can replace counting with some I AM affirmation.. or Powerful Visualizations that take the same amount of time as these counts. In other words, the timing can easily become intuitive.

However, it may end up being all you can handle for the first months of this new program to do but one repetition of this breath work (as its influence could be remarkable) but as you become more adept and familiar with this power, you will certainly be able to handle more. There are other breath exercises that you may employ as warm-ups to this sacred power breathing exercise, and here are a few warm-ups that you may practice for 15 or 30 minutes at a time (or longer, when you choose to later on). Don't be 'bashful'.. practice all you like.

Sit still in a straight back position, breathe in normally through your nose four separate times, not shallow, and not big.. but like a normal breath – and then on the fifth time that you inhale, you inhale a very large and very expansive breath. And on its exhale make it a blasting cleansing release. Get out ALL the air in your lungs. DO this 5 Level exercise as described on 5 Separate Repetitions. This will take you a bout 2 to 3 minutes to complete the 5 repetitions.

Next sitting still in a straight back position place your finger on your right nostril depressing it firmly, and breathe in through the left nostril fully, fully, fully – so your lungs are filled up by just the left nostril intake. Then *without a pause or rest depress the left nostril and EXHALE through the right nostril till your lungs are empty, empty, empty. Really Empty.* Then without a pause or a rest keep holding down the left and Inhale in through the right nostril. Then when your lungs are Filled with just the right nostril breath, depress the right nostril again and release it all fully, fully through the left nostril. It is just a Two Way Reverse Exercise. Very Simple.

But…if you do this for 20 to 40 minutes or longer you will be amazed at how and what you feel. And when you pray and meditate during these exercises it becomes very powerful indeed. Remember you are purifying body and cells of all the impurities that come in and find lodging over the course of a lifetime. You are also cleansing your mind of ego tendencies, bad habits, weaknesses in your will, and many more things than we can name. Do it with enthusiasm and humility. *This is a high-speed way to achieve dominion of the ego and the fleshly weaknesses we may have.* You are taking in the Holy Breath-Spirit, and it is having its wonderful, cleansing "way with you". These exercises are given as an opportunity to practice the Breath for its benefits. For some, transformative spiritual technologies like these are familiar, but others may not have been exposed to them before. Although, the sacred power breath-exercise in this chapter may be new to many people. It definitely deserves our attention and application. Enjoy and prosper in it.

"HAHM -- HAH" "Hiss -- Hah"

Please know this. One will find a heavenly calming peaceful pleasure in sitting back with closed eyes to simply breathe deeply and rhythmically. And one will feel the need to shut down one's thoughts and present mental activity. To achieve this just go to *Hahm-hah* some call it *His-Hah*. It is really the "sound" of our breath going in and out. This is a secret to quieting the mind. We "focus" on this sound, to the exclusion of thinking. Just the sound. To quiet the mind, attend to the Sound.

Remember, *Consciousness is the Masculine aspect of Divine Being* ...where all planning, designing and meditation occur, on the *what and the why* for our life experience. *The Feminine aspect of the Divine is the Breath and Breathing*. But know this. This Divine Feminine is not "just our breath". WE tend to think of our breath as a kind of nothing. '*It's just that we need oxygen*' we think. No it is our very life and awareness. This Divine Breath is the intelligence in the universe. It has consciousness in IT too. When participating here we are in a creative, restorative, healing, constructive – **particle by particle, detail by detail-PROCESS-oriented activity**...but it is often and mostly in silence. Meditation is Masculine, Breathing is Feminine.

Breathing is experiential spirituality. Breathing says *I love you*. Breathing actually *melts your ego processes right away from you*. Breathing purifies us, above everything else in the universe. The Breath makes us Christ-like.

Meditation *is introspective, worshipful spirituality*. Meditation says *I honor you, I do and I will listen endlessly*. Meditation is being one with the Divine masculine mind. Breath work is being one with the Divine feminine Breath/Pneuma/Spirit of the cosmos. Enjoy them both.

Sacred Power

Meditation *is introspective, worshipful spirituality.*
Meditation says *I honor you, and will listen
endlessly.* Meditation is being one
with the Divinely masculine Mind.

Splendorous Light Within

Mystic Traveler
I, II, III

Mystic Traveler is a 21st century quintessential film story on the entire life of Jesus. His family of nine members, four brothers [*named in the gospels*] 2 sisters and his deep affectionate Essene parents Joseph and Mary are all there. His great uncle Joseph of Arimathea, plays a key role also. It is a marvelous exposition on Jesus' development, his nature and his personal qualities in 1st century Gallilee. We witness how he becomes Earth's prime spiritual trailblazer and *Anointed One* of Israel. His great uncle Joseph, a wealthy tin trader-businessman, teaches Jesus much and often – taking him on journeys in business travels to many countries on 3 continents: *Europe,* the *mid-east* and the *far-east.* On these journeys over the years we see his personality congeal through remarkable adventures in honing his personal and spiritual awareness. Witnessing the formative *Trials and Tests that advance Elders* within the Essene spiritual Sect *[of his family]* his spiritual *Initiations* allow us to see him evolve before our eyes. His precocious spiritual-scriptural awareness is startling as he "**confounds the teachers of the temple with his wisdom."** As a master of matter-energy, today's amazing film effects reveal All his healing Powers and Abilities like no film before. Finally, the spiritual principles he teaches the *common people* are presented with a down to-earth mystic wisdom that benefits all by introducing their inner light. With Old Testament flashbacks and startling new *historic and scientific facts* we bring you a film never before imagined. Prepare to be astounded. by the unknown Christ!

SCRIPT SAMPLE:
Scene from Mystic Traveler III

On the hillside where he feeds multitudes of people, an unconscious Mary Magdalen is brought on a stretcher to Jesus. He heals her of seven diseases and discusses with her secrets of the Divine Mind. We see him travel through a community dealing with large numbers of followers.

                      MARY MAGDALEN

Since I was young I was interested in spirituality but…all the priests or rabbis I knew.. seemed not.. sincere. They didn't have that loving Authority or... power. I may've expected too much. But it made them hollow…they seemed..emptier...than regular people. (Jesus nods a little)

But YOU talk about being in relationship with the infinite invisible. How did...how does someone…Well, I know God exists..that's why we..and the universe exist but.. how did you Do it? Why does the Infinite Being respond to YOU?

                      JESUS

Very good question. No one's ever asked me that before… not even my teachers. The answer's so simple, you may marvel at its simplicity. See.. everything comes from God's mind...especially Love and communication. Why should we think God is far away? God is the closest presence in our life and our feelings. He's 'closer than breathing and nearer than hands and feet.' And...the Infinite Invisible, being Mind...lives infinitely, in all this.. mostly, as a service To US. But our heart and mind IS God's perception of Earth. Our hurts and pains are God's hurts and pains. Our Love is God's. Our talents are God's. Our dreams God's dreams. Our family is God's family. Our prayers God's prayers. I felt if we love feeling affection God must also. All Attributes come from God right? (She smiles)

So I felt his presence in my mind and emotion. In effect..I did feel God, IN me. I felt this Other observing awareness in _my_ mind..in my actions, emotions, and life…because I was Looking for it. It's so lightly felt. I thought.. that sharing My words and emotions with Him-Her was a Reciprocal pleasure...in moment-to-moment living.

See…many folks pray to God from duty...guilt…or out of Habit. But..sharing real time and Love in conversation with God is a tender Partnership, so well… even an Invisible Being responds to whole hearted affection…

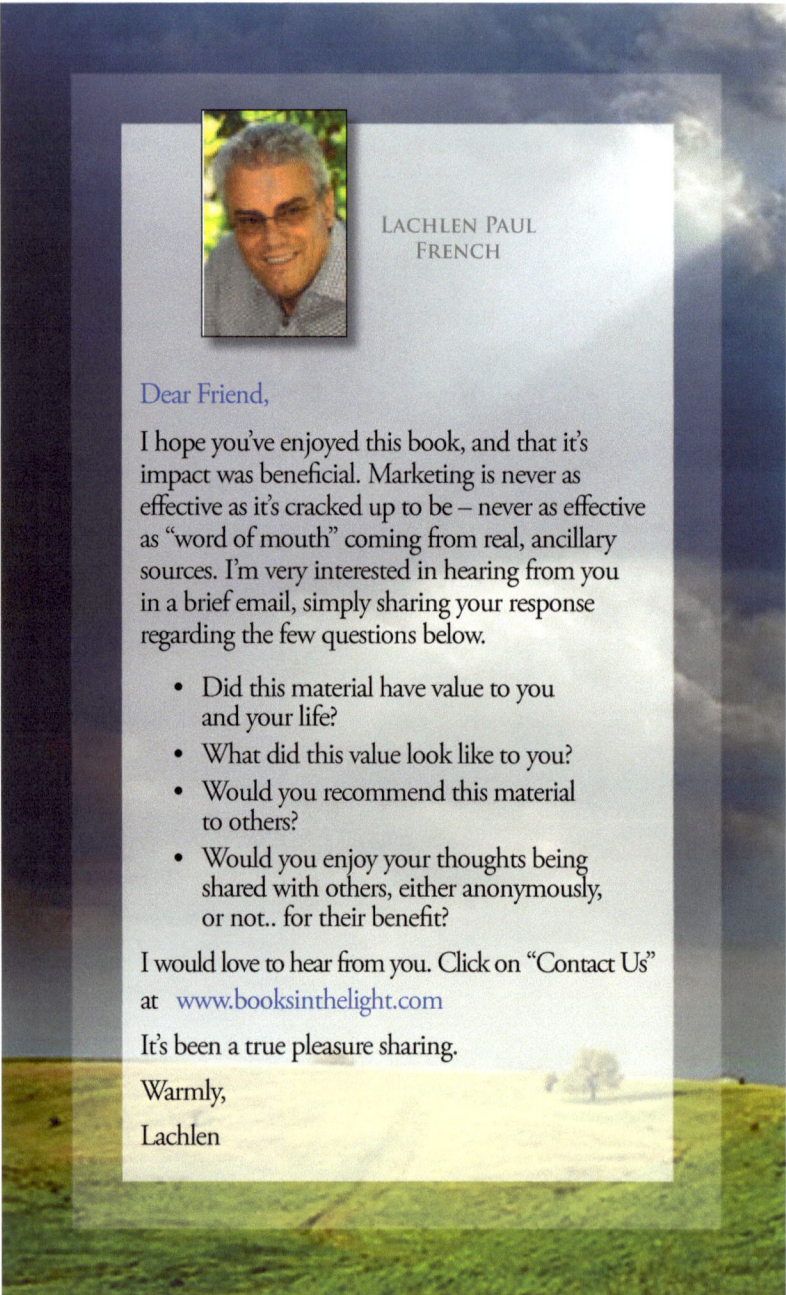

Lachlen Paul French

Dear Friend,

I hope you've enjoyed this book, and that it's impact was beneficial. Marketing is never as effective as it's cracked up to be – never as effective as "word of mouth" coming from real, ancillary sources. I'm very interested in hearing from you in a brief email, simply sharing your response regarding the few questions below.

- Did this material have value to you and your life?
- What did this value look like to you?
- Would you recommend this material to others?
- Would you enjoy your thoughts being shared with others, either anonymously, or not.. for their benefit?

I would love to hear from you. Click on "Contact Us" at www.booksinthelight.com

It's been a true pleasure sharing.

Warmly,

Lachlen

About the Author

Attending university at a School of Theology as a ministerial Seminarian he degreed in Theology, Comparative Religion and Homiletics at Ambassador College in California. Communications, Psychology and Science were also his within his degree program. A champion racquetball player in university, he also played quarterback. After receiving his Theology and Communications degrees he entered the Master's Program in Communications and Fine Arts at the USC studying under director John Houseman. He then taught Speech Communications at university in Public Communication, Persuasion and Oral Interpretation. Coming from a theatrical family he annually wrote, produced and directed college *stage-entertainments* that were consistently praised. He preached as well.

Splendorous Light Within is a product of decades of biblical, scientific, historical research, and a love of esoteric instruction which Christ and the Essenes gave to their disciples. Scholars understand well that there's a large amount of information not being told to the masses. This book and his others **Breath of Light** along with his book *on **Thomas***. his screenplays ***Mystic Traveler*** on Christ's life, all tell a story of Jesus, that is not being told to the public. This new information turns over the soil of the old story and gives the most accurate verifiable data right now.

Working nine years on rendering into modern language that ancient *Gospel of Thomas*, the author finally brings it to the public, finishing almost two decades of writing. Having been deeply involved in the inner endeavors for spiritual Self-awareness, his has been a path of private exploration into the experiential domain of divine consciousness and the universal breath (unfortunately known as 'spirit' in the Bible) which is the actual message in the Judeo-Christian Bible. When it's known, it all becomes new. He has been teaching and writing over decades. He has lived these disciplines taught by the ancient spiritual programs he studied – a fact rarely heard anymore. These ideas were variously taught in the Mystery disciplines as Paul called them, and were offered by such as the Essenes-Christianity, the Gnostics and many ancient and eastern sources as well. Alongside this he spent three decades in a pure passion and deep absorption in the science of Quantum Physics – the science able to unite Physics and Metaphysics and Mathematics with Consciousness.

With his love of quantum science, an insightful vision is given regarding the mystery of the omnipresent cosmic energy that comprises everything-everywhere (even our own Life force–Consciousness). The Author's correlation in the science of the Quanta, "packets of light essence" allows us to see why reality and consciousness meld at the deepest levels of our being and also in the universe. It's why scientist's expectations *affect* the outcome of their *quantum experiments*. It's *bothered* them for a century.

Years later the author spent time with the world famous spiritual author, *William Samuel,* and even discovered they were related. He called William his spiritual mentor.

Coming from a centuries-old family of writers he felt a deep call to write in other forms. As an author-screenwriter of metaphysical high-concept adventures his screenplays *Mystic Traveler I-III* present *Christ's entire life –* even the missing years and finally **Aquarian Effect** – depicts *life in the 21st century* after 2012. His non-profit humanitarian firm, Synergy Services Foundation and his film-production firm, Aquarian Entertainment LLC were founded for these purposes. They bring healing educational service-endeavors to uplift our day to day living.

Early on he was the public speaking voice of the Barksdale Self-Esteem Foundation in California, delivering seminars through the state on developing and living true self-esteem. He started three business service firms and was involved with one of the three businesses that he started, going Public.

Today he remains a writer and enthusiastic public speaker in metaphysical, spiritual awareness, including the realm of film making. He lives with his belov'ed. His children are on their own bright satisfying pathways.

www.ingramcontent.com/pod-product-compliance
Lightning Source LLC
Chambersburg PA
CBHW041610220426
43668CB00001B/1